Halfway THERE

Also by Norm Foster

Bedtime Stories
Dear Santa
Ethan Claymore
A Foster Christmas
The Foster Season
The Foursome
The Gentleman Clothier
Hilda's Yard
Jasper Station
Jenny's House of Joy
Jonas and Barry in the Home
Kiss the Moon, Kiss the Sun
The Ladies Foursome
The Long Weekend
The Melville Boys
Mending Fences
Ned Durango (with Leslie Arden)
Office Hours
Old Love
On a First Name Basis
One-Actmanship
Opening Night
Outlaw
Self-Help
Sinners
Skin Flick
Storm Warning
Triple Play
The Writer
Wrong for Each Other

Halfway THERE

NORM FOSTER

Playwrights Canada Press
TORONTO

LIBRARY AND ARCHIVES CANADA CATALOGUING IN PUBLICATION
Title: Halfway there / Norm Foster.
Names: Foster, Norm, 1949- author.
Description: A play.
Identifiers: Canadiana (print) 20210139358 | Canadiana (ebook) 20210139374 | ISBN 9780369102225 (softcover) | ISBN 9780369102232 (PDF) | ISBN 9780369102249 (HTML) | ISBN 9780369102256 (Kindle)
Classification: LCC PS8561.O7745 H35 2021 | DDC C812/.54—dc23

Playwrights Canada Press operates on Mississaugas of the Credit, Wendat, Anishinaabe, Métis, and Haudenosaunee land. It always was and always will be Indigenous land.

We acknowledge the financial support of the Canada Council for the Arts, the Ontario Arts Council (OAC), Ontario Creates, and the Government of Canada for our publishing activities.

Canada Council for the Arts | Conseil des arts du Canada
ONTARIO ARTS COUNCIL
CONSEIL DES ARTS DE L'ONTARIO
an Ontario government agency
un organisme du gouvernement de l'Ontario
Canada
ONTARIO CREATES | ONTARIO CRÉATIF

For my children, Lee, Randy, Daniel, and Jacqueline.

Halfway There was first produced from August 10 to 27, 2016, at the Foster Festival in St. Catharines, Ontario, with the following cast and creative team:

Vi: Lisa Horner
Rita: Sheila McCarthy
Mary Ellen: Helen Taylor
Sean Merrit: Darren Keay
Janine Babineau: Kirsten Alter

Director: Patricia Vanstone
Stage Manager: Carolyn Mackenzie
Set and Costume Design: Sue LePage
Lighting Design: Chris Malkowski

Cast of Characters

Janine Babineau, mid to late thirties
Vi
Rita
Mary Ellen
Sean Merrit, forty-two years old

Vi, Rita, and Mary Ellen can be anywhere from fifty to sixty years old

Time

The present. Friday afternoon.

Place

A restaurant called Junior's in the town of Stewiacke, a town in Nova Scotia located halfway between the equator and the North Pole.

Act One

SCENE ONE

There are tables and a counter with stools in the diner. On the front door is sign on a string. The sign, facing the audience, reads "Closed." Lights up to reveal three women, VI, RITA, *and* MARY ELLEN *sitting at a table in the diner.*

RITA: Well, I don't know why she doesn't just leave him. They don't even sleep in the same bed anymore.

VI: Get out.

RITA: Hand to God, Vi. She sleeps in the master bedroom and Ian sleeps in what used to be Harvey's room.

VI: Harvey? Their son Harvey?

RITA: Yep.

VI: So, why don't they just get a divorce?

MARY ELLEN: No, Elspeth won't do that.

RITA: No. She says it would be too hard on the children.

VI: Harvey and Glad?

RITA: Right.

VI: Harvey's forty-one.

RITA: But he only just moved out a couple of months ago. He's still finding his legs. His parents divorcing could be a setback. Plus there's the whole circumcision fiasco. That muddies the waters too.

VI: The circumcision has nothing to do with Harvey's insecurities.

MARY ELLEN: The "botched" circumcision.

RITA: Performed by Elspeth's veterinarian cousin.

VI: Oh, that's just a rumour. I don't think it was done by a veterinarian at all.

MARY ELLEN: Elspeth swears it's the gospel.

RITA: I wouldn't have let him near a flank steak with a knife let alone a you-know-what. My land, it's no wonder Harvey is skittish.

MARY ELLEN: I've never seen a man flinch so much around cutlery.

VI: But he was a baby when it happened.

RITA: Yes, but those things stay with a person. That's why I'm against circumcision. It should be outlawed.

VI: And Glad? Glad lives in Costa Rica last I heard.

MARY ELLEN: Well, not so much lives as is "in custody."

RITA: Anyway, I hope they work it out. I mean, Elspeth just turned sixty. She hasn't got too much tread left on those tires.

VI: I'm just glad I didn't have any kids when I got divorced. Johnny's girl Katie still finds it tough, and he's been divorced from her mother for twelve years.

MARY ELLEN: How old is she now?

VI: Seventeen. And she's having a rough go of it up there in Thunder Bay. Hanging with a bad crowd too. Johnny's really worried.

RITA: Johnny's a cop. Can't he tell the cops up there to keep an eye on her?

VI: He has. But it's not the same as being there himself.

MARY ELLEN: It's so hard being a teenager these days. I hope she gets through it.

VI: From your lips to God's ears, Mary Ellen. All right, girls, I'm off to the gym. Or as the owner insists on calling it, Dugan's Pub.

MARY ELLEN: No, don't go yet, Vi. What's the rush?

VI: I'm meeting Johnny for happy hour.

RITA: Oh, Johnny. What's Johnny?

MARY ELLEN: Yeah, what's Johnny?

VI: We meet every Friday at Dugan's for happy hour. You know that.

MARY ELLEN: So, he can't wait on you for fifteen minutes?

RITA: Yeah, you know what they say about keepin' a man waiting.

VI: No. What do they say, Rita?

RITA: It makes him want you more.

MARY ELLEN: Maybe Rita has a point, Vi. Maybe you should play hard to get.

VI: Mary Ellen, I've already been got. I've been got six ways from Sunday.

RITA: She's right. Her gettin' got days are long gone.

VI: Well, now I haven't stopped gettin' got. I still get got. There's just no need to play hard to get got. Now, I gotta get. The love of my life is waiting.

SEAN Merrit enters the restaurant.

I suppose he can wait fifteen more minutes.

VI sits.

MARY ELLEN: Well, what do we have here?

RITA: What do we have, indeed?

SEAN: Ladies.

VI: Well, the jury's still out on that but thank you anyway.

MARY ELLEN: Vi, stop that.

(to SEAN) Don't listen to her. She's nothing but trouble.

RITA: And so am I if you like that sort of thing. And I hope you do.

MARY ELLEN: Now, that's enough, you two.

(to SEAN) They're a caution. I'm sorry.

SEAN: Quite all right.

MARY ELLEN: Just sit anywhere. Janine will be out shortly.

SEAN: Janine?

VI: Your waitress. She's using the facilities at present.

SEAN: Oh. Thank you.

SEAN sits.

RITA: Well, he's a handsome rascal, isn't he?

VI: You can say that again.

MARY ELLEN: Not from around here, I'm guessing.

VI: Oh, he's not from around here at all, Mary Ellen. He's from away as sure as a monkey's got a bare arse.

MARY ELLEN: He is a cute one.

RITA: He is. And looks to be unspoiled. Like a piece of fresh fruit on a sturdy vine. Just waiting to get plucked.

SEAN: Ladies. I can hear you.

RITA: Oh, we know, dear. We don't like to talk behind someone's back.

VI: No, we'll say it straight to your face.

SEAN: Well, that's good to know.

MARY ELLEN: So, were we right? Are you from away?

VI, RITA, and MARY ELLEN move to SEAN and sit, surrounding him.

SEAN: From away? Uh . . . yes, yes I am. I just got into town and I haven't eaten since breakfast. That's why I stopped in here.

RITA: Oh, ya poor thing. You gotta eat. You gotta keep up your strength. You need it for your endurance. Although I'll bet your endurance is just fine. Is it?

VI: What's your name?

SEAN: Sean Merrit.

VI: Well, welcome to Stewiacke. I'm Violet. This is Rita. And this is Mary Ellen.

SEAN: Pleased to meet you.

VI: So, where are you from, Sean?

SEAN: Toronto.

VI, RITA, and MARY ELLEN just stare at SEAN.

What's wrong?

MARY ELLEN: We don't like Toronto.

RITA: We don't like Toronto one bit.

SEAN: That seems like an odd reaction. Is there a reason that you don't like Toronto?

MARY ELLEN: Oh, there's a very good reason.

VI: Mary Ellen's niece Martine fell in love with a fella from Toronto.

MARY ELLEN: Fell head over heels.

RITA: Like a ton o' bricks.

VI: Next thing you know she gives up a good job at the Scoop and Save and moves to Toronto to be with him. Oh he promised her the world he did. And I don't mean little trinkets and baubles here and there. No, I mean he literally promised her the world.

SEAN: Well, I don't think he could "literally" promise her the world. I mean, "literally" would mean . . .

VI: Who's telling the story here, Sean?

SEAN: Sorry. Go ahead.

VI: So, within two months he decides that he's not "in love" with Martine anymore. He said she had some qualities that weren't apparent to him at first blush. Qualities that only came to light when they moved in together.

SEAN: Like what?

VI: Well, when she got mad she'd throw knives at him.

MARY ELLEN: Not big knives. Not your carving knife or your bread knife.

RITA: No, just little ones. A paring knife or a cheese knife.

VI: But that wasn't the worst of it.

SEAN: Throwing knives at him wasn't the worst of it?

RITA: No. Martine is a kleptomaniac. She steals things. She can't help herself.

VI: And they were living in a small apartment and they had no place to put everything.

RITA: And apparently this got to be too much for the jam tart Toronto boyfriend. I guess he doesn't like clutter. And so he sent her packing. Without so much as a by your leave.

VI: He broke that poor girl's heart he did.

MARY ELLEN: Broke it bad.

VI: And she comes back home with tears in her eyes and her tail between her legs. And I mean literally with her tail between her legs.

Pause.

Okay, now I'm messin' with ya'. She doesn't have a tail.

RITA: At least not one long enough to tuck between her legs.

The women laugh.

SEAN: And that's why you hate Toronto?

VI: That's it.

SEAN: Well, that's tarring a pretty sizable population with the same brush, isn't it?

VI, RITA, and MARY ELLEN just stare at SEAN.

But it's probably valid. You're probably right.

RITA: So what brings you to Stewiacke, Sean? Is there a slacks convention in town?

SEAN: I'm going to be working at the medical clinic. I'm taking over for Doctor Caldwell for a month.

RITA: You're a doctor?

SEAN: I am.

RITA: Well. And me about due for my annual physical. How fortuitous.

MARY ELLEN: Yes, I think I might be coming down with something.

VI: I'm feeling a little feverish myself, girls. Whoo! Is it hot in here or is it him?

RITA: So, you're taking over for Pooch Caldwell?

SEAN: Pooch?

RITA: Yeah, Pooch. We've called him that for years.

SEAN: Do I want to know why you call him that?

RITA: Well, it's no big secret. A while back we had a pharmacist here named Virginia Wilmot. Sometimes she'd go out for lunch and not come back for two or three hours. She'd just disappear. So one day the druggist asked her where she'd been and she said nowhere. She was just screwin' the pooch. Turns out it was Doctor Caldwell.

VI: That wasn't the biggest revelation though.

SEAN: No?

VI: No. It was the fact that it took two or three hours.

RITA: We all thought a little better of Pooch after that.

SEAN: Are you sure there's a waitress working here?

VI: Yeah, she's here. Give her time. She's experiencing a heavier period than usual this month.

MARY ELLEN: I don't know if Janine would want you telling Sean that, Vi.

VI: Why not? He's a doctor.

MARY ELLEN: I know, but maybe Sean doesn't want to hear about her heavier period. He just landed in town. He's looking for a sandwich and a beverage. Maybe it's too soon to talk about menstruation.

VI: Is it too soon to talk about menstruation, Sean? Because if it is, I'll shut the hell up.

SEAN: Not at all. Talk about whatever you like.

RITA: Where do you stand on circumcision?

MARY ELLEN: Rita!

RITA: He said talk about whatever you like.

SEAN: Maybe I should find another restaurant.

VI: Oh nonsense. Stay right where you are. Here, let me start you off with a coffee.

VI goes behind the counter and gets the coffee pot and pours a coffee for SEAN.

SEAN: No, I'm in kind of a hurry, so . . .

VI: Oh, nobody's in a hurry here.

SEAN: No?

MARY ELLEN: We can't be. Every time you go out you see somebody you know and you wind up talking to them for half an hour. Nobody gets anywhere in a hurry here.

RITA: Oh, that reminds me. I saw Penny Steeves on the way to work this morning.

MARY ELLEN: Really? I haven't seen Penny in weeks.

RITA: She's been over in Elderbank looking after her father.

MARY ELLEN: Ted?

RITA: Yeah.

MARY ELLEN: What's wrong with Ted?

RITA: He's got the gout. Can barely get around.

VI: It's the whiskey that causes it. Isn't that right, Sean?

SEAN: That can be one of the causes, yes.

VI: Well, that's what it is with Ted. That man drinks like a winded goat.

MARY ELLEN: Drinks likes he's trying to forget two wives.

SEAN: That much, huh?

MARY ELLEN: Oh that much and more.

RITA: So, yay or nay, Sean? On the circumcision question.

JANINE Babineau enters from the back.

JANINE: She-it!! This is a bad one. It is one giant motherffff . . .

The other three women point to SEAN.

Hey, how you doin'? I hope you haven't been waiting long. I was just . . . out back.

RITA: It's okay, Janine. Vi told him about your heavy flow this month.

JANINE: *(to VI)* You what?

VI: He's a doctor. It's fine.

JANINE: You what?

RITA: He didn't even blink, Janine. Took it right in stride.

VI: Okay, I really have to go. Janine, you're coming to Dugan's when you get off?

JANINE: Dugan's? Uh . . . yeah. Sure.

VI: We'll save you a seat then. What about you, Mary Ellen? You coming tonight?

MARY ELLEN: No, I gotta go home and feed the brood.

VI: Oh for the love of God. Let them get their own supper for a change. You've got two grown boys and a man-child husband. Surely they can forage for something on their own.

MARY ELLEN: Sorry. Next week for sure though.

VI: Rita?

RITA: Oh, I'll be there. What the hell else have I got to do on a Friday night? Unless the doctor here would like to check me for lumps.

VI: Sean? Nice meeting you.

MARY ELLEN: Yes, nice meeting you, Sean. Good luck at the clinic.

SEAN: Thank you.

RITA: Yes, I'll be stopping by to see you for sure. Tell me, do you have an "after hours" policy? It doesn't have to be at the clinic. It could be at my place. Or in my car.

VI: Rita, come along with ya. Bye, Janine!

MARY ELLEN: Bye, Janine!

JANINE: Bye.

RITA: Bye, Sean.

SEAN waves to RITA. VI, RITA, and MARY ELLEN exit.

SEAN: Charming women.

JANINE: I'm sorry about the "heavier flow" talk.

SEAN: No problem.

JANINE: What can I get you?

SEAN: Can I see a menu?

JANINE: Okay, but if you want food, you're going to have to order fast. We close in twenty minutes.

JANINE hands SEAN a menu.

SEAN: You close at five?

JANINE: We sure do.

SEAN: But that's the supper hour. Isn't that your busiest time?

JANINE: No. Most folks go to the Cavalier for supper. Or to Dugan's. Our business is mainly breakfast and lunch. Besides, Junior likes to go home and have supper with his family.

SEAN: Oh, that's nice.

JANINE: It is.

SEAN: And it gives you time to have supper with your family too, I guess.

JANINE: I don't have a family.

SEAN: No?

JANINE: Nope. Just me. I live with a fella but he's off working out west on the oil sands. Eight weeks on, two weeks off.

SEAN: Eight weeks, huh? That's a long time to be away from your loved ones.

JANINE: I didn't say I loved him. I said I lived with him. So, what'll you have?

SEAN: Oh. I haven't even looked yet.

JANINE: Well, hurry up. Junior'll be shuttin' off the stove soon.

SEAN: What would you recommend?

JANINE: I'd recommend going to Dugan's. But if you must eat here then I'd go with the chicken Caesar.

SEAN: All right. The chicken Caesar it is.

JANINE goes to the kitchen door and calls in.

JANINE: Junior? I need a chicken Caesar out here, please.

(to SEAN) That shouldn't be more than a few minutes.

SEAN: Thank you.

JANINE: So, the girls said you're a doctor?

SEAN: Yes. I'm here for a month filling in for Doctor Caldwell. I'll be here until the long weekend.

JANINE: What happened to Doctor Caldwell?

SEAN: He's going to South America to do missionary work.

JANINE: Pooch is? He didn't tell me that. Pooch is my doctor. Course, I haven't been to see him in a year. Maybe that's why he didn't tell me.

SEAN: A year? You must be due for a physical then. You should make an appointment.

JANINE: For a physical?

SEAN: Yes.

JANINE: My my, you don't waste any time, do you?

SEAN: Pardon me?

JANINE: In town ten minutes and you want to see me naked already.

SEAN: No, I didn't mean it like that.

JANINE: I'm kidding. So, where are you from?

SEAN: Toronto.

JANINE: Oh, we don't like Toronto.

SEAN: Yes, I heard.

JANINE: And where are you staying while you're here?

SEAN: I'll find a hotel, I guess.

JANINE: There aren't any.

SEAN: Any what? Hotels?

JANINE: No.

SEAN: There are no hotels here?

JANINE: No. Where do you think you are? Tatamagouche? We've got a bed and breakfast though. Luanne's. Just up the road.

SEAN: Well, maybe I'll try there then.

JANINE: So you drove all the way from Toronto without knowing where you were going to be staying when you got here?

SEAN: Well, coming here was kind of a last-minute decision.

JANINE: Ah. Interesting.

SEAN: So, I noticed that sign out on the highway that read "Halfway to the North Pole." What does that mean?

JANINE: Stewiacke is exactly halfway between the equator and the North Pole.

SEAN: Really?

JANINE: It's our claim to fame.

SEAN: That's funny.

JANINE: Why is that funny?

SEAN: No, I don't mean that it's funny about it being your claim to fame. I just mean . . . I recently split up with my fiancée. So, a month ago I had it made. A woman I loved. A future together. A good medical practice. And now here I am, sitting in a diner, halfway to the North Pole. I guess that's an indication of how far I've fallen in a month.

JANINE: It doesn't sound like you're flattering us.

SEAN: I'm sorry. It's nothing about your town. It's just . . . never mind. I'm sure it's a lovely town.

JANINE: It'll do.

SEAN: Are you from here?

JANINE: I am. Born and raised.

SEAN: You never had an urge to move away? See what's out there?

JANINE: Well, I'm not an idiot. I know what's out there. That's why I'm here. I've been to New York, Montreal, Los Angeles, Paris, Milan . . .

SEAN: Paris and Milan?

JANINE: Yeah. I used to be a buyer for a clothing store. I got the job when I graduated from the London College of Fashion.

SEAN: The London College of Fashion. Wow. So, you've been to all those places and you came back here? Why?

JANINE: I missed the life here. And I missed my friends.

SEAN: Your friends?

JANINE: Yeah.

SEAN: Violet, Rita, and Mary Ellen? Those friends?

JANINE: Yeah. And others. I've got plenty of friends in town.

SEAN: But you could make new friends.

JANINE: I don't want new friends.

SEAN: Why not?

JANINE: Because the old friends aren't broken.

SEAN: Hmm. You're uh . . .

JANINE: I'm what?

SEAN: You're an interesting woman.

JANINE: I am, aren't I? You, on the other hand, have a bit of a hangdog personality.

SEAN: Hangdog?

JANINE: A little woebegone, yes.

SEAN: Is that how I appear? Oh, that's pathetic. All right. No more of that. And thank you for bringing it to my attention.

JANINE: We speak our minds here.

SEAN: I'm learning that. So, I guess your parents were happy that you moved back home after being away.

JANINE: No, as soon as I left home they packed up and moved away themselves.

SEAN: Where did they go?

JANINE: Toronto. Yeah, Stewiacke isn't for everybody, but those of us who stay love it.

SEAN: Well, I believe that when you find a place that feels like home, that's where you should be.

JANINE: Have you found that place yet?

SEAN: I thought I had.

JANINE: Until your fiancée dumped you.

SEAN: I didn't say she dumped me. I said we split up.

JANINE: Because she dumped you.

SEAN: Yeah.

JANINE: You ever been married before?

SEAN: Nope. This was going to be the first and last time.

JANINE: Really? You've never been married at your age? What are you, forty-six? Forty-seven?

SEAN: Forty-two.

JANINE: Wow. This last month really has been hard on you.

SEAN: What about you? Have you ever been married?

JANINE: Nope.

SEAN: At your age? You've gotta be . . .

JANINE: Careful.

SEAN: So, why have you never married?

JANINE: I haven't found the love of my life yet.

SEAN: What about the guy you're living with?

JANINE: Oh Bradley and I get along okay, and I suppose I love him a bit, but the love of my life? No, that's a whole different level. But there's a certain comfort in being with Bradley. There's something to be said for that, right?

SEAN: Comfort?

JANINE: Yeah.

SEAN: I'd be looking for a little more than comfort if I were you. Comfort isn't love. Comfort doesn't excite you. Comfort is a pair of slippers.

JANINE: Yeah, well at least I have a pair. Sorry.

SEAN: Maybe we should change the subject.

JANINE: Good idea.

SEAN: How long have you worked here?

JANINE: Ever since I moved back. Eight years now.

SEAN: What about your friends? What do they do?

JANINE: Rita works at the bakery across the street. Mary Ellen teaches preschool. And Vi's an accountant. She works out of her home.

SEAN: Well, they're a delightful trio.

JANINE: They're great gals. They usually stop in here at around four o'clock every day for a little gabfest. It's something I really look forward to.

SEAN: You know that heavy flow of yours could be a symptom of a bigger problem. I'm not saying it is, but it could be.

JANINE: Like what?

SEAN: Oh, uterine fibroids, polyps, dysfunction of the ovaries. Any number of things. Maybe you should come and see me next week.

JANINE: Uh . . . sure, I could do that. I'm off Wednesdays.

SEAN: Well, how about next Wednesday morning? I'll run some tests.

JANINE: Okay.

SEAN: What's your last name?

JANINE: Babineau.

SEAN: Janine Babineau. I'll pencil you in for Wednesday morning then.

He looks at his watch.

Oh boy. I'd better get that salad to go.

JANINE: Really?

SEAN: Yeah. I've got to check in at the clinic before they close for the day.

JANINE: Okay.

She moves to the kitchen door and shouts.

Junior, put some legs on that salad!

(to SEAN) So, what happened to your practice?

SEAN: Pardon me?

JANINE: When you were whinging about your sorry existence a minute ago you said you had a good medical practice. What happened to it?

SEAN: Well, there were three of us in this small neighbourhood clinic. Myself, my fiancée, and a doctor named Lorenzo. So, when my fiancée and I split up we figured it would be impossible to work together so one of us had to go.

JANINE: Uh-huh. And why you?

SEAN: It was the gentlemanly thing to do.

JANINE: Your fiancée was sleeping with Lorenzo.

SEAN: How did you know?

JANINE: The man's name is Lorenzo. He's probably better looking than you. More exciting than you. Knows how to dance really well. No, you didn't stand a chance.

SEAN: Is dancing that big a deal?

JANINE: To a woman? Very big deal. There's something sexy about a man who knows how to dance.

SEAN: Really?

JANINE: Oh, very sexy. You don't dance?

SEAN: Never learned how.

JANINE: Well there you go. I don't know why she agreed to marry you in the first place.

We hear a bell ring from the kitchen.

There's your salad.

JANINE exits to the kitchen.

SEAN: *(to himself)* I don't know if he was better looking than me.

JANINE enters with a bag containing the salad.

JANINE: Oh he was. Here you go.

SEAN: Thank you. What's the damage?

JANINE: No, it's on me. Consider it a welcome to Stewiacke.

SEAN: Really?

JANINE: Absolutely.

SEAN: Well, thank you. That's very kind.

JANINE: Don't mention it.

SEAN: So, I'll see you on Wednesday.

JANINE: Yes you will.

SEAN starts to exit and then stops.

SEAN: Listen, maybe you'll let me repay you by buying you dinner next week.

JANINE: What?

SEAN: For the salad. Let me buy you dinner next week.

JANINE: Buy me dinner?

SEAN: Yes.

JANINE: Well, that would be awkward, wouldn't it? I mean, Wednesday morning I'm in your examination room, naked, and later that night we're eating baba ghanouj like you never even saw it.

SEAN: Saw what?

JANINE: Me. Naked.

SEAN: Oh.

JANINE: No, that would be too weird.

SEAN: Yeah, I guess it would be weird.

JANINE: Very weird.

SEAN: We could go to dinner Tuesday night. Before the examination.

JANINE: Same thing. Tuesday night we shake hands good night, and Wednesday morning? Boom! I'm naked again.

SEAN: You're right. We would have to let a suitable amount of time pass between the examination and the dinner.

JANINE: Isn't this unethical on a couple of levels?

SEAN: Why?

JANINE: Well, first of all, I told you I'm living with a guy.

SEAN: Well, this is just dinner. Repayment for you giving me the salad.

JANINE: And secondly, should a doctor be dating a patient?

SEAN: Again, it's not a date. It's just dinner.

JANINE: That's a date. Dinner is a date.

SEAN: Dinner is a date?

JANINE: Dinner is a date.

SEAN: Oh. All right, let's forget it.

JANINE: I think we should.

SEAN: I wasn't hitting on you, by the way. I wasn't making a pass. I wouldn't do that with you.

JANINE: Why not? What's wrong with me?

SEAN: Nothing. I just didn't want to appear inappropriate. You're living with a guy. A comfortable guy. And for me to make a pass at you would be very inappropriate. Besides, it's too soon for me to start dating just yet. So soon after . . . you know?

JANINE: Getting dumped.

SEAN: Thank you.

JANINE: All right, look. Come to Dugan's tonight and you can buy me a beer.

SEAN: A beer?

JANINE: Yes. To repay me for the salad.

SEAN: Oh. Okay.

JANINE: Good.

SEAN: So a beer's not a date?

JANINE: A beer's not a date. A beer is just . . . "Hey, lemme buy you a beer." That's all a beer is.

SEAN: Oh. Okay.

JANINE: Good.

SEAN: Even if it's pre-arranged?

JANINE: What?

SEAN: Well, we're making plans for me to buy you a beer at Dugan's. That's pre-arranged. Isn't that a date?

JANINE: Oh my God.

SEAN: Well, if we're planning on meeting somewhere for a beer, that's a date. That's what a date is. Making plans to be together somewhere. That's a date.

JANINE: Okay. Twelve ninety-nine.

SEAN: What?

JANINE: For the salad. Twelve ninety-nine. Let's have it.

SEAN: You're making me pay?

JANINE: I'm making you pay.

SEAN: Oh. Okay.

SEAN reaches into his pocket and takes out money.

Twelve ninety-nine?

JANINE: Twelve ninety-nine.

SEAN: The menu said it was ten ninety-nine.

JANINE: I'm charging you extra for mental cruelty.

SEAN hands her the money.

SEAN: There's fifteen. Keep the change.

JANINE: Yeah, that was happening anyway.

SEAN gets halfway out the door and stops.

SEAN: So, I'll see you tonight then?

JANINE: What?

SEAN: For the beer. Are we still on?

JANINE: Uh . . . Yeah. Okay. Fine.

SEAN: And it won't be a date. I'll just walk in and act surprised that you're there and I'll say, "Hey, lemme buy you a beer."

JANINE: Get out.

SEAN: Right.

SEAN exits. JANINE turns the sign around so now, from the inside, it reads "Open." Lights down.

SCENE TWO

Time: the following Friday.

Place: the same.

Lights up to reveal MARY ELLEN, RITA, *and* VI. *The diner is closed. The sign on the door, from the inside, reads "Open."*

RITA: So, I was in the parking lot and I was walking towards my car and he walked right up behind me and he said, "Rita"? And I turned around and there he was in all of his priestly glory. Draped in black from head to toe except for the white collar shinin' out at me like a beacon of purity. And I said, "Yes, Father?" And he says, "Why do you and your friends call me Father What-A-Waste"?

VI: He did not!

RITA: I swear he did.

MARY ELLEN: Oh my God!

VI: How did he find that out?

RITA: He must have overheard us. I don't know.

VI: Sweet beloved. So what did you say?

RITA: I told him the truth.

MARY ELLEN: Rita, you did not!

RITA: I did! I says, "Well, Father, you are the handsomest man in Stewiacke by a long shot. I mean, you put the rest of these boys to shame," I says. "And yet you've taken a vow of celibacy. Well, me and the girls think that's a terrible waste of manpower. Hence the name Father What-A-Waste."

MARY ELLEN: And what did he say to that?

RITA: Well, he grinned and he blushed and he said, "Well, that's a relief. I was worried it was because you thought my sermons were a waste of time." And I said, "Oh no, I don't listen to your sermons, Father. I just like to watch your lips move."

VI: Oh, you devil!!

RITA: I did!

The women laugh. JANINE enters from the kitchen. She carries a birthday cake with a few candles on it. She sings happy birthday. VI and RITA join in.

JANINE, VI, & RITA: "Happy birthday to you. Happy birthday to you. Happy birthday, Mary Ellen. Happy birthday to you."

MARY ELLEN: Oh, you girls.

VI: Happy birthday, dear.

MARY ELLEN: Thank you. And here I thought you all might've forgotten.

JANINE: Now, when have we ever forgotten a birthday amongst the four of us?

MARY ELLEN: Well, never, but there's always a first time. Isn't this just wonderful? Thank you.

RITA: All right, make a wish and blow out the candles.

MARY ELLEN blows out the candles immediately.

Mary Ellen, I said make a wish.

MARY ELLEN: I did.

RITA: That quick? You didn't even think about it.

MARY ELLEN: I didn't have to think about it. It's the same wish I make every year.

VI: And what's that?

MARY ELLEN: That the four of us will be together and be best friends for another whole year.

RITA: Oh my Jesus, girl. That's the loveliest thing I ever heard.

VI: I think I might cry.

JANINE: Now, why would you wish something like that, Mary Ellen? Of course we'll be together and be best friends.

MARY ELLEN: Well, I started doing it when you moved back home after being away for those ten years.

RITA: Yes, that was thoughtless of you, Janine, goin' away like that.

VI: Well, she's always been the thoughtless one.

JANINE: Hey, I came back, didn't I?

MARY ELLEN: And ever since then I've been making that same wish. And so far it's come true every year. Now who else can say their birthday wish comes true every year?

VI: My God, I love you, Mary Ellen. You are the salt of this earth, I swear.

VI hugs MARY ELLEN.

MARY ELLEN: I love you too, Vi. Now where are my presents?

RITA: Presents?

JANINE: Oh, presents. We forgot about that.

VI: That's right. We did. Sorry.

MARY ELLEN: No birthday presents?

JANINE: Nope.

MARY ELLEN: Awww.

JANINE: Not until tonight at Dugan's.

MARY ELLEN: Dugan's?

RITA: We're throwing a little party for you. Starts at eight o'clock. We figured you might want to go home and have supper with your boys on your birthday. That's why we're not starting until eight.

MARY ELLEN: Oh. Well, that was good thinking.

VI: So, what did Kyle and the boys get you?

MARY ELLEN: Well, they haven't given me my presents yet. They'll probably do that at supper. But they gave me breakfast in bed this morning. Yes, they did. And they put a single red rose in a little vase and put it right there on the tray. It was like being in a fancy hotel.

JANINE: Oh, that is so nice.

MARY ELLEN: It was lovely. I felt like a queen.

RITA: And you deserve to feel like a queen, Mary Ellen. You're a saint. You're much nicer than the three of us are.

MARY ELLEN: I know I am, love. That goes without saying.

JANINE: All right. Come on, let's have some cake.

VI: Just give me three small pieces, Janine. One big piece will put me off my diet.

RITA: Are you dieting again?

VI: For two weeks now.

RITA: And what have you lost?

VI: At last count, about fourteen days.

JANINE cuts the cake and gives each woman a piece.

MARY ELLEN: So, who's going to be at my party tonight?

JANINE: Well, you and Kyle. Vi and Johnny. Rita. Rita, have you got a date?

RITA: Not yet. But I've still got three hours.

JANINE: Me. Rachel Coy and her new boyfriend.

VI: Rachel's got a new boyfriend?

RITA: Tom Sweeney.

VI: Tom Sweeney? Isn't he going out with . . .

RITA: It's over.

VI: Tom and . . .

RITA: Done.

VI: Don't tell me those rumours were . . .

RITA: Every one of them.

VI: So, she was . . .

RITA: Twice a week as it turns out.

VI: Over at the . . .

RITA: Right there in the office. Every Tuesday and Thursday.

VI: Well, I'll be damned.

JANINE: I don't know Tom. Where's he from?

VI: He's from Stewiacke.

RITA: No, he's from Milford. He says he's from Stewiacke so he'll sound sophisticated.

MARY ELLEN: How's Bradley doing, Janine?

JANINE: He's fine. He called last night. We talked for about fifteen minutes.

RITA: Was it phone sex?

MARY ELLEN: Oh, Rita, stop it.

RITA: What? He's been away for a couple of weeks now.

JANINE: It wasn't phone sex.

MARY ELLEN: You see?

JANINE: Phone sex takes a good half-hour. No, we just talked. About nothing really.

VI: That's the sign of a solid relationship. When you talk about nothing.

JANINE: It is?

VI: Oh yeah. Me and Johnny talk about nothing all the time. In fact, if we ever talked about something, I'd think that we were drifting apart.

MARY ELLEN: But by talking you get to know each other a little better.

VI: We know each other well enough, believe me.

RITA: Vi's right. I'll tell you, nothing kills a relationship faster than intimacy. Two people getting too close to one another.

VI: I agree.

JANINE: Really?

VI: Oh God, yes. When Johnny and I first moved in together I was in the bathroom one morning brushing my teeth and he strolls right in, walks over to the toilet and starts doing his business.

JANINE: No!

VI: He did.

MARY ELLEN: Kyle does that too. I hate that.

VI: Me too. So, I says, "What in the hell are you doing?" And he says, "What does it look like?" And I says, "It looks like you're relieving yourself, but you can't be because I'm still in here." Good Lord, I don't need to see that. And I don't want him to see me going through my morning ablutions either. We don't need to see everything, for pity's sake. And we don't need to talk about everything. Sometimes people in a relationship just need to shut up.

MARY ELLEN: I disagree. I like talking about something. I like having meaningful conversations once in a while.

JANINE: Do you and Kyle have meaningful conversations?

MARY ELLEN: No. The fact is most of my meaningful conversations happen right here. With you girls.

RITA: Well, that's men for you. You can't talk to them even if you wanted to.

VI: Well, they've got nothing to say.

RITA: Bunch of dim-wits.

SEAN appears at the door. He carries a manila envelope. He tries to open the door but it's locked. He knocks.

VI: Oh, it's the new doctor.

RITA: So it is. Hi, Sean!!

VI: Hi, Sean!!

RITA: He is handsome, isn't he?

VI: Oh, he's a doll, Rita.

VI waves at SEAN.

Hi!!

SEAN points down at the doorknob.

MARY ELLEN: I think he wants in.

RITA: Do you think?

MARY ELLEN: Well, he's pointing at the doorknob.

RITA: Oh, that's what he's pointing at. I thought he was flirting.

JANINE moves to the door and opens it.

JANINE: It's after five. We're closed.

SEAN: Oh. I'm sorry.

MARY ELLEN: Invite him in, Janine.

VI: Yeah, invite him in.

JANINE: Okay. Come on in. We're having a little birthday celebration for Mary Ellen.

SEAN: Oh. Happy birthday.

MARY ELLEN: Thank you.

SEAN: *(to JANINE)* No, I was just on my way home and thought I would stop in with the results of your examination.

JANINE: Oh, you didn't have to do that. Unless I'm dying. Am I dying?

SEAN: No, you're not.

JANINE: Then sit down and have some cake. Did you hear that, girls? I'm not dying.

VI, RITA, and MARY ELLEN cheer.

SEAN: Listen, I can come back some other time.

JANINE: No, sit. Sit.

RITA: Yeah, take a load off, Doc. Come on.

RITA pulls a chair up close to her.

SEAN: Oh, well, thank you. I suppose I can have a small piece of cake.

JANINE cuts a small piece of cake for SEAN.

VI: How's everything over at Luanne's bed and breakfast, Sean? Are you comfortable?

SEAN: Oh very comfortable, yes.

VI: Good. Luanne's a dear heart.

SEAN: She's very nice.

VI: And the flatulence doesn't bother you?

SEAN: The what?

VI: Luanne's flatulence problem. That doesn't bother you?

RITA: Well, of course it doesn't bother him. He's not sleeping with her. Or are you?

SEAN: No, I'm not.

RITA: There. You see? It wouldn't be a problem at all.

VI: Well, he could happen upon a lingering fragrance by accident.

RITA: Have you done that, Sean?

SEAN: No. It's been fine.

RITA: You see? It's been fine.

VI: She is such a dear heart.

JANINE: There you go.

JANINE puts a piece of cake in front of SEAN.

SEAN: Thank you.

(to MARY ELLEN) I hope you don't mind me intruding on your birthday party.

MARY ELLEN: No, not at all. The more the merrier.

VI: Besides, the real party isn't until tonight at Dugan's. You're welcome to come to that too if you like.

SEAN: At Dugan's? Well . . . uh . . . maybe I will. Is everybody going to be there? I'm mean, the four of you?

VI: We sure are. Ooh, Rita. Here's your date.

SEAN: What?

VI: You can be Rita's date.

RITA: Oh, that's a good idea.

SEAN: Your date?

VI: Yeah. Rita's got no one to go with tonight.

RITA: So, what do you say, Sean? You wanna be my date? I can pick you up.

SEAN: I'm living two doors down from the pub.

RITA: Doesn't matter. I'll still pick you up. It'll be the shortest most memorable car ride you ever had.

SEAN: Uh . . . well . . .

MARY ELLEN: Oh say yes, Sean. Rita won't bite.

RITA: Not so fast there, Mary Ellen.

VI: It'll help you put that broken heart behind you.

SEAN: Who said I have a broken heart?

JANINE raises her hand.

VI: Yes, we heard all about Lorenzo and about how much happier your fiancée . . . what's her name?

SEAN: Rebecca.

VI: Right. We heard about how much happier Becky is with Lorenzo. Especially with the whole dancing thing.

SEAN: Dancing?

VI: Becky loves the way Lorenzo dances. Apparently you're not much of a dancer. That's what we heard.

SEAN: I didn't say that.

VI: Well, I heard it from someone.

JANINE raises her hand.

Oh, there you go. I heard it from Janine.

RITA: I can teach you how to dance, Sean.

MARY ELLEN: Oh, Rita is a champion dancer. She won a dance contest in Dartmouth last year.

VI: Well, she didn't do it alone, Mary Ellen. There was a pole involved.

RITA: Vi, cut it out.

(to SEAN) I took ballroom lessons for three years.

MARY ELLEN: She's the best dancer in the whole town.

RITA: So, what do you say, Sean? Are you gonna be my date tonight or not?

SEAN: . . . Well . . .

RITA: Oh come on. Pull that rod out of your ass and be a sport.

SEAN: . . . Okay, sure. I'll be your date, Rita.

RITA: Good. I'll pick you up at eight.

SEAN: I'll be ready.

RITA: Oh, and one more thing. There are those who would say that just because I asked you out I'm easy.

SEAN: . . . And?

RITA: Nothing. That's it. I was finished.

MARY ELLEN: Well, I'd better get home. I want to see what my men got me for my birthday.

VI: Yeah, I'd better go too. Johnny and I are going out to dinner before the party.

JANINE: Where are you going?

VI: Dugan's.

JANINE: But that's where the party is.

VI: Yep. It's your one-stop celebration centre.

JANINE: Oh, Mary Ellen, your niece Martine was in here for breakfast this morning.

MARY ELLEN: Salt and pepper shakers again?

JANINE: No, this time it was a juice glass.

MARY ELLEN: I'll tell her to bring it back.

JANINE: Thank you.

RITA: Eight o'clock, Sean. And wear something pretty, okay?

SEAN: Will do.

RITA: See you tonight, Janine.

VI: Bye now.

JANINE: Bye, girls.

VI, RITA, and MARY ELLEN exit.

(to SEAN) So, you've got a date tonight.

SEAN: Looks like.

JANINE: Ooh. Sean and Rita sittin' in a tree. K-i-s-s-i-n-g.

JANINE goes about cleaning up after the women, picking up their dishes and putting the cake away.

SEAN: So why doesn't Rita have anyone in her life?

JANINE: Oh, she had someone once. She got married young. At nineteen to a guy named Jason. They had a son, Shane, but he died in a snowmobile accident. He and his father went through the ice when Shane was only nine and the boy drowned. The marriage didn't survive either. They got divorced shortly after. And now?

Well, she gets involved with men but only up to a point, and then she backs off. I fully expect Rita will be alone the rest of her life.

SEAN: That's too bad.

JANINE: It is too bad. She's a great woman. Smart, funny, sexy. I'd like to see her find someone to share that with. Hey? Maybe it'll be you. Maybe you two will hit it off on your big date tonight.

SEAN: Fingers crossed.

JANINE: All right then, let's have it.

JANINE holds out her hand.

SEAN: Have what?

JANINE: The envelope. My results.

SEAN: Oh, right. Yeah. Well, we didn't find anything really. I suspect your problem was due to anti-inflammatories. Are you taking any?

JANINE: For my back. I'm on my feet all day and sometimes that catches up with me.

SEAN: Exactly. Well, I'm sure that's all it was.

JANINE: Okay. Good to know.

SEAN: Yes, you're as fit as a fiddle.

JANINE: Isn't it odd for a doctor to deliver the results to a patient at her place of work?

SEAN: No. I mean you're on my way home.

JANINE: Oh.

SEAN: That's all it is.

JANINE: But usually a nurse would call to make a follow-up appointment and you'd tell me then, right?

SEAN: Usually. But, like I said, you're on my way home.

JANINE: Uh-huh. Well, can I see them?

SEAN: See what?

JANINE: The results.

JANINE holds out her hand.

SEAN: Oh! The results, yes. Well, I just told you what they were.

JANINE: Well, as long as you brought them along, I might as well see them.

SEAN: Of course. Yes. But there's something I want to tell you first.

JANINE: And what's that?

SEAN: I can't be your doctor anymore.

JANINE: What?

SEAN: I can't be your doctor. You'll have to find someone else.

JANINE: Why?

SEAN: There's a conflict of interest.

JANINE: What conflict of interest?

SEAN: I find you attractive.

JANINE: You what?

SEAN: I find you attractive. I'm attracted to you. And that makes it impossible for us to have the proper doctor–patient relationship.

JANINE: You find me attractive?

SEAN: Yes.

JANINE: Oh. Eww.

SEAN: What's wrong?

JANINE: So when you were examining me on Wednesday, you were . . . eww.

SEAN: No, there was nothing eww about it. It was strictly professional.

JANINE: But you were attracted to me.

SEAN: Yes.

JANINE: During the exam. When I was naked.

SEAN: I put it out of my mind.

JANINE: How?

SEAN: I thought of something else.

JANINE: Like what?

SEAN: Neil Young.

JANINE: Neil Young?

SEAN: Yes.

JANINE: The singer Neil Young? From Crosby, Stills, Nash, and Young?

SEAN: Yes. And also from his successful solo career.

JANINE: Why would you think of him?

SEAN: Because I'm not attracted to Neil Young. I don't find Neil Young physically arousing.

JANINE: Oh. Eww!

SEAN: No, there's no eww! Thinking of Neil Young while I'm examining you negates the feelings I have for you.

JANINE: Completely?

SEAN: Completely.

JANINE: Why not David Crosby?

SEAN: What?

JANINE: David Crosby is far less attractive than Neil Young. Why wouldn't you think of him?

SEAN: I don't think David Crosby is less attractive than Neil Young.

JANINE: You don't?

SEAN: No. He's less attractive than Graham Nash.

JANINE: Well, who isn't?

SEAN: But not Neil Young.

JANINE: What about Stephen Stills?

SEAN: I don't even know what he looks like.

JANINE: But wait now. You're finished here in another three weeks.

SEAN: So?

JANINE: So, why are you telling me that you're attracted to me? Chances are I'm not going to have another appointment with you before you leave, so you didn't need to tell me.

SEAN: That's true.

JANINE: So why did you?

SEAN: I wanted you to know how I felt about you. I didn't want to leave without telling you that.

JANINE: Are you going off to war?

SEAN: No.

JANINE: Then what the hell?!

SEAN: I told you in case you felt the same way and wanted to get it out in the open.

JANINE: Oh.

SEAN: So, do you?

JANINE: Do I what? Feel the same way?

SEAN: Yes.

JANINE: No.

SEAN: Oh.

JANINE: No I don't.

SEAN: Got it.

JANINE: Not at all.

SEAN: Good. The first no did the trick.

JANINE: I mean, you're a good-looking man. There's no denying that.

SEAN: Thank you.

JANINE: You're no Graham Nash.

SEAN: Well, who is?

JANINE: But I'm living with a guy.

SEAN: Right. Bradley.

JANINE: Exactly.

SEAN: Who you don't love. You just live with.

JANINE: I love him a little bit.

SEAN: Uh-huh. A little bit. Ooh that'll scare me off. She loves him a little bit. I don't stand a chance.

JANINE: Look, Sean, you've got a lot going for you. You're a doctor, you seem like a nice guy . . .

SEAN: All right, you don't have to start listing all of my attributes.

JANINE: Actually, I was done.

SEAN: You were?

JANINE: A doctor and a nice guy. That's the list.

SEAN: All right, but I still think you've left the door open for me. You love him a little bit? That's not slamming the door shut. That means there's hope. A chance that you and I might become involved.

JANINE: Do you want me to respond to that?

SEAN: Not if you don't want to, no.

SEAN waits for JANINE to respond. She doesn't.

Okay. Well, I'm going to leave now before this gets awkward.

JANINE: *Before* it gets awkward?

SEAN: Goodbye.

JANINE: Wait.

SEAN: What?

JANINE: Can I see the results?

SEAN: The what?

JANINE: The results of my examination. The envelope.

SEAN: Oh, this envelope is empty. See?

He opens up the envelope and shows JANINE.

Nothing.

JANINE: Why is it empty?

SEAN: I was just using it as an excuse to drop by. I thought it would look more official.

JANINE: Oh.

SEAN: We never take files out of the clinic.

JANINE: That would be unprofessional.

SEAN: Exactly. I'll see you tonight.

JANINE: Tonight?

SEAN: Mary Ellen's birthday party.

JANINE: Oh. You're still going to that?

SEAN: Why wouldn't I?

JANINE: Well, this—what just happened here—was kind of embarrassing for you. I thought maybe you'd want to stay home and avoid the public shaming.

SEAN: No, not at all.

JANINE: No?

SEAN: No. I've been embarrassed way worse than this.

JANINE: Really?

SEAN: Way worse.

JANINE: Wow.

SEAN: So, yeah, I'll be there tonight.

JANINE: Well, I admire your daring.

SEAN: Hey, that's number three.

JANINE: Pardon me?

SEAN: On my list of attributes. Daring makes three.

JANINE: Get out.

SEAN: Right.

SEAN exits. Lights down.

SCENE THREE

Time: the following Monday.

Place: the same.

Lights up. The diner is closed. JANINE *is behind the counter holding the coffee pot.* VI, RITA, *and* MARY ELLEN *are sitting there, thinking.*

They each have an empty coffee cup in front of them. There is silence for a few moments as the women think.

RITA: Neil Young, huh?

JANINE: That's what he said.

JANINE *brings the coffee pot to the table and pours coffee for the women.*

RITA: The old Neil Young or the young Neil Young?

JANINE: I don't know.

RITA: I'd do the young Neil Young. I wouldn't do the old Neil Young. I'd do the old Graham Nash.

VI: Well, who wouldn't?

MARY ELLEN: So, he's attracted to you?

JANINE: Yes. And he wants us to become involved.

RITA: That must be why he didn't make a move on me at Mary Ellen's birthday party.

VI: Could be that.

RITA: Oh, I'm sure it was. I mean, he was the perfect gentleman. He made polite conversation all evening, kept his hands to himself, and didn't try to kiss me good night. It was the worst date of my life.

VI: I've got an appointment with him next week. I'd better not hear him singing "Heart of Gold."

MARY ELLEN: *(to JANINE)* So, what are you going to do about it?

JANINE: I'm not going to do anything about it.

MARY ELLEN: You don't like him?

JANINE: Sure I like him. But I'm living with a guy.

MARY ELLEN: Right. Bradley.

JANINE: That's right.

VI: And what if you weren't living with a guy?

RITA: Oh, there's a good question.

VI: Well?

JANINE: Well, I don't know.

RITA: Well, there's your answer.

JANINE: How is that my answer?

RITA: You're unsure. You haven't completely dismissed the idea. If you weren't living with Bradley you would go out with the doctor and before long you'd be having babies with him.

MARY ELLEN: Is that what she said? I don't think she said that.

RITA: Oh, Mary Ellen, wake up. A year from now they'll be married and using the bathroom together.

JANINE: I think you're way off the mark, Rita.

RITA: We'll see. He'd be a real catch though, Janine. Good looking. A doctor. That's two out of three.

MARY ELLEN: What's the third?

RITA: Can he cook.

MARY ELLEN: Oh. I thought you were going to say sex.

RITA: Oh hell no. I can look after that myself. But a man who can cook for you? That's the pot of gold at the end of the rainbow.

VI: Speaking of men and women and their relationships.

MARY ELLEN: . . . Yes?

VI: Well, last night we were lying in bed and Johnny asked me to . . . you know?

MARY ELLEN: Oh, Kyle asks me to do that every night.

VI: No. He asked me to marry him.

JANINE: What?

VI: He did.

MARY ELLEN: Right out of the blue like that?

VI: Like he was asking me to pass the potato salad. You could have knocked me over with a feather.

MARY ELLEN: Wow.

VI: So, what do you think?

RITA: I think I'd rather do what Kyle asks Mary Ellen to do.

VI: Come on. This is a marriage proposal. It's a pretty big deal.

JANINE: Congratulations, Vi.

MARY ELLEN: Yes, congratulations indeed.

VI: Thank you. I said no.

JANINE: You said no?

VI: Turned him down flat.

JANINE: Why?

VI: Because I don't know if I'm ready for marriage.

MARY ELLEN: Nobody's ready for marriage. We just take a leap of faith. That's all it is.

RITA: You did the right thing.

VI: Really?

RITA: How long have you and Johnny been living together?

VI: Nine years.

RITA: Right. So if you don't get married, who cares? You're together and you're in love. That's all that matters.

VI: Exactly. And I'm worried that marriage might change us. I've always thought that our relationship remained interesting and exciting because we weren't married. We were together because we wanted to be. Not because a piece of paper said we had to be.

MARY ELLEN: Oh honest to God, Vi. The piece of paper doesn't say that at all. It just says who you married, where you were married, and who married you. Believe me, I know. I've been checking mine trying to find a loophole.

RITA: So, what did Johnny say when you turned him down?

VI: He got mad. And we had a big fight. And then he stormed out and went over to his brother's place to sleep.

RITA: No.

VI: Yeah. And then he came back an hour later. He said he missed me.

JANINE: Oh my God, Vi, if you don't marry that man, I will.

VI: He's a good one, isn't he?

JANINE: He's the best.

RITA: You're a lucky girl, Vi. You and Johnny have got an ideal relationship.

MARY ELLEN starts to cry.

JANINE: Mary Ellen? What's wrong?

MARY ELLEN: Nothing. I'm just happy for Vi.

JANINE: Mary Ellen?

MARY ELLEN: Really. That's all it is. I'm very happy for you, Vi. That Johnny is one of a kind.

VI: Yeah. So, maybe I'll marry him after all. Who knows?

MARY ELLEN cries.

JANINE: Mary Ellen, what is wrong with you? And don't say you're happy for Vi. No woman gets that happy because another woman's got a good man. Now what is it?

MARY ELLEN: I didn't get anything for my birthday.

JANINE: What?

MARY ELLEN: Kyle and the boys. They didn't get me anything for my birthday.

RITA: You mean they forgot it.

MARY ELLEN: No, they didn't forget it. They just didn't think it was important enough to make a fuss over. When I got home that evening they gave me a birthday card. One birthday card signed by the three of them and that was it. There was no cake. No presents. I even made the supper that night.

VI: Well, what about breakfast in bed? You said they made you a nice breakfast in bed with a rose on the tray and . . .

MARY ELLEN: There was no breakfast. There was no rose. There was nothing. I just told you that because I was embarrassed that I wasn't being made to feel special on my birthday by my own family. I swear it just about killed me. I cried all day.

JANINE: Oh, sweetheart.

VI: That's men for you.

RITA: That's men all right.

VI: They can be such selfish, obtuse jackasses.

RITA: They're a bunch of idiots.

VI: I'm glad I've got Johnny because the rest of them are as worthless as a meat thermometer at a vegetarian cook-off.

SEAN appears at the door. He tries it. It's locked. He knocks.

Oh, look. It's Sean. Hi, Sean!!

RITA: Hi, Sean!

VI: Isn't he adorable?

SEAN points to the doorknob.

RITA: I think he wants in. He's pointing to his crotch again.

VI: Let him in, Janine.

JANINE: No.

VI: Why?

JANINE: Because we're in the middle of a crisis here with Mary Ellen.

VI: Oh, right. I'm sorry, Mary Ellen.

MARY ELLEN: No, no, no. My pity party is over. Time to mcve on.

RITA: Are you sure, dear?

MARY ELLEN: Yes. We've spent enough time on me. God knows it was all of two minutes. Let the man in.

JANINE opens the door.

JANINE: Hi, Sean. Come on in.

SEAN: I always seem to show up just after you close.

RITA: Are you here to ask me out on a second date? Because I put out on the second date.

VI: Rita, stop that.

RITA: Oh, I'm just kiddin'.

She mouths "no, I'm not" to SEAN as she shakes her head no.

SEAN: Actually, I'm here to talk to Janine.

VI: Oh. Did you bring more test results with you? You're not carrying an official envelope this time.

SEAN: No, I didn't come here to talk about anything medical.

VI: Oh, is that right? Did you hear that, girls? The doctor wants to talk to Janine about a non-medical issue. I wonder what that could be.

RITA: Probably something private. Personal.

MARY ELLEN: Well pull up a chair then, Sean. Gather round, girls.

VI: Yes, pull up a chair. What is it you want to talk about?

SEAN: Well, like Rita said, it's . . . it's personal.

The four women stare at SEAN *for a moment.*

VI: Go on.

SEAN: When I say personal, I mean I would like to keep it between Janine and myself.

VI: Oh fine. I can take a hint.

MARY ELLEN: Yeah, I guess I should be getting home anyway.

RITA: Why?

MARY ELLEN: Well, because I've got . . .

RITA: You've got what?

MARY ELLEN: I've got . . .

RITA: You've got an ungrateful family waiting for you to cook for them. And then clean up after them. Is that what you've got?

MARY ELLEN: Mostly.

RITA: Well, not tonight, Mary Ellen. No. Tonight I'm taking you out.

MARY ELLEN: Out where?

RITA: I'm taking you to the Cavalier for dinner.

MARY ELLEN: The Cavalier?

RITA: We'll have a fine meal and we'll have some wine and I'm going to ask them to put a single red rose in a vase right there in the centre of the table. How does that sound?

VI: It sounds good to me. I'm coming too.

JANINE: Me too.

RITA: What do you say, Mary Ellen?

MARY ELLEN: I say you girls mean the world to me. Thank you. But we'll have to dress up if we're going to the Cavalier. And that means I would have to go home and change. And Kyle will be there and I'll have to explain where I'm going.

RITA: Don't worry about it. Come to my place. I'll find a dress for you.

MARY ELLEN: Wear one of your dresses?

RITA: Sure. Why not?

MARY ELLEN: Well, the dresses I wear say I'm a married woman. The dresses you wear say open for business.

VI: Oh, come on, Mary Ellen. Live a little.

MARY ELLEN: No. You know what? I'm going to go home and get changed. And I'm going to tell Kyle exactly where I'm going and that he and the boys can fend for themselves or starve to death. And not just tonight, but any damned night that I don't feel like cooking from now on. So, there you have it. We'll meet at the Cavalier in one hour.

RITA: Done.

JANINE: All for one!

RITA: And one for all!

VI, MARY ELLEN, and RITA start for the door.

VI: We're off then. Oh, Mary Ellen, Martine came to see me with a tax question this morning.

MARY ELLEN: Your stapler again?

VI: Three-hole punch.

MARY ELLEN: I'll tell her to bring it back.

RITA: Goodbye, Sean.

SEAN: Goodbye. Enjoy your dinner.

RITA: Oh we will.

VI: Bye, Sean.

SEAN: Bye.

VI sings the first line of Neil Young's "Heart of Gold."

RITA and MARY ELLEN join in as the three women exit.

VI, MARY ELLEN, and RITA exit.

SEAN: Neil Young. Nice. You told them.

JANINE: There are no secrets in Stewiacke, Sean.

SEAN: Well, there could be if you people made an effort.

JANINE: So, what's on your mind? What's so personal that you can't discuss it in front of the girls?

SEAN: Well, here's the thing. I'm going to Halifax this weekend. I've never been there before so I thought, what the heck? I'll drive in Friday evening and come back Sunday.

JANINE: Sounds good. Halifax is a great city. I think you'll enjoy it.

SEAN: I would like you to come with me.

JANINE: What?

SEAN: As a tour guide. That's all.

JANINE: A tour guide?

SEAN: Yes.

JANINE: You want me to spend the weekend with you in Halifax? As your tour guide?

SEAN: Yes. It will be completely innocent. We'll see the sights, have dinner. Whatever you want to do.

JANINE: Go dancing?

SEAN: Dancing? Uh . . . no. But on Saturday night there's a production of *Romeo and Juliet* we could go to.

JANINE: Wow. The theatre. You're going to make my head spin. And what would the sleeping arrangements be for the weekend?

SEAN: I'd get us separate rooms.

JANINE: Separate rooms. I see.

SEAN: So, what do you think?

JANINE: Well, first of all, I'm not buying the tour guide thing. I wasn't born yesterday. We're back to you wanting to start a relationship with me again.

SEAN: Yes we are.

JANINE: Oh. You admit it?

SEAN: Why waste time? Let's just dive right into the sexual tension.

JANINE: There is no sexual tension.

SEAN: There is over here.

JANINE: Sean, you're on the rebound. That's not a good way to begin a relationship.

SEAN: I am not on the rebound.

JANINE: You have a photo of your ex-fiancée in your examination room!

SEAN: Okay, that minor detail aside, if a person meets someone he likes and it happens to be shortly after a breakup, should he ignore his feelings just because he might be on the rebound? No, I say. Nay. Thou shant denyest thy feelings. T'would be ill-advised.

JANINE: You are cute, I'll give you that.

SEAN: You're thinking about it. That's good.

JANINE: What makes you say that?

SEAN: The first word out of your mouth wasn't "no."

JANINE: Well, the answer is no because I work on Saturday.

SEAN: Is that the only reason you won't go? That's even better.

JANINE: Why is that better?

SEAN: Because the reason wasn't Bradley.

JANINE: But the reason should be Bradley.

SEAN: But it wasn't. So, can you get Saturday off? I'll ask for you. Junior??!!

JANINE: Stop that.

SEAN: Junior? Janine wants desperately to go to Halifax with me. Can you give her Saturday off!!?

JANINE: Cut it out! He's not even back there. He went home fifteen minutes ago.

SEAN: I know. I passed him on my walk down here.

JANINE: Well, well, well. You've got a sense of humour. I haven't seen that before now.

SEAN: It was buried under a mudslide of hurt.

JANINE: And you write country songs too.

SEAN: So what do you say?

JANINE: Look, I'm flattered, Sean. I really am, but . . .

SEAN: Wait! Don't answer yet.

JANINE: Why not?

SEAN: Because I can sense a "no" coming. Take twenty-four hours to think about it.

JANINE: But I already know my answer.

SEAN: Then take twenty-four hours before you say it out loud. Seriously. Give me your answer tomorrow.

JANINE: It'll be the same answer tomorrow as it is right now.

SEAN: But that'll give me a twenty-four-hour reprieve before my heart is broken again.

JANINE: Wow. That was good.

SEAN: Thank you.

JANINE: That was very good.

SEAN: Are you impressed?

JANINE: Beyond impressed.

SEAN: Then my work is done here.

JANINE: Yes, and you'll be leaving on a high note.

SEAN: Always leave them wanting more.

JANINE: Well, I don't know if I'm wanting more.

SEAN: You don't want more?

JANINE: I think my cup is full.

SEAN: All right, I'll see you tomorrow.

JANINE: You will, sir. Yes.

SEAN: And you'll think about Halifax?

JANINE: More than I ever have.

SEAN: Good. I can't wait to hear what your answer will be.

JANINE: I already told you what it will be.

SEAN: Shh! No. Don't spoil the surprise.

JANINE: There is no surprise.

SEAN: Enough! Speak no more, fair maiden. And so I say good night. Good night. Parting is such sweet sorrow.

JANINE: Get thyself out.

SEAN: Right.

SEAN exits. Lights down.

Act Two

SCENE ONE

Time: The next day. Tuesday.

Place: the same.

Lights up to reveal RITA *pouring herself a coffee. The sign on the door facing the audience now reads "Closed." The diner is open.* JANINE *enters from the kitchen followed by* VI.

VI: Why didn't you tell us this at dinner last night?

JANINE: Last night was Mary Ellen's night. I didn't want to inject my problems into that.

RITA: So he wants to take you to Halifax. As a tour guide.

VI: He wants to get you into bed, that's what.

JANINE: He said we would be in separate rooms.

VI: Oh, well, that'll put a stop to any shenanigans then. Yes. No one has ever had sex staying in separate rooms at the same hotel because nobody's ever had too much to drink and given into temptation before!

RITA: So, what are you going to do?

VI: She's going to say no, of course.

RITA: Why is she going to say no?

VI: Two words. Brad ley. She's already got a man. A good man. Why would she put that relationship in jeopardy for a weekend fling with a good-looking, well-to-do, single, vulnerable doctor? And here I am talking my*self* into liking the idea. Jesus, Mary, and Joseph! Look, Janine, you're the baby of our group. We look out for you. And I say you shouldn't go.

JANINE: Vi, nothing will happen.

VI: So you're going?

JANINE: I didn't say that.

RITA: So, you're not going.

JANINE: I didn't say that either.

VI: You mean you're thinking about it? You're actually thinking about it?

JANINE: I might be.

VI: I can't believe this.

JANINE: Why are you becoming so indignant?

VI: Because I thought better of you, Janine. Of the four of us, you've always been the clearest thinker.

RITA: I thought that was me.

VI: Oh please.

(to JANINE) And now you're thinking of cheating. That's not clear thinking at all.

JANINE: I'm not thinking of cheating. I would just be going to Halifax with the guy.

VI: And would you tell Bradley about it?

JANINE: Probably not.

VI: Then that's cheating. You don't have to have sex to cheat. Right, Rita?

RITA: No, but it's more enjoyable that way.

VI: The mere fact that you're deceiving your partner—going somewhere with some other guy for sex or not—that's cheating.

JANINE: I don't think of Bradley as my partner.

VI: You live together.

JANINE: Yeah, I know, but we have separate bank accounts, we each pay our own bills. We buy our own food. The only thing we share is space.

VI: Why would you live with a guy if you don't consider him your partner?

JANINE: For the company, I guess. I don't know.

VI: My God, Janine. I didn't know you were so indifferent where relationships are concerned. So laissez-faire. Did you pick this attitude up when you travelled to all those European cities? Because I don't think you could pick it up here.

JANINE: Are you offended, Vi? Does my attitude offend your moral core? Is that what this is?

VI: I just thought better of you.

JANINE: Stop saying that. You've got no reason to think less of me unless I think less of myself, and I don't. So stop saying that.

VI: Fine. I won't voice my opinion then.

JANINE: No, I want you to voice your opinion. I value your opinion. I just don't want the judgment that comes along with it.

VI: You value my opinion?

JANINE: Of course I do. I value all of your opinions. Rita's, Mary Ellen's. I need those voices in my life.

VI: Fine. No more judgment then.

JANINE: Thank you.

VI: You slut.

The women laugh. MARY ELLEN *enters.*

MARY ELLEN: Hello!

RITA: Mary Ellen. You're late. Oh, by the way, Martine came into the bakery this afternoon.

MARY ELLEN: Loaf of bread?

RITA: The tip jar.

MARY ELLEN: I'll tell her to bring it back.

RITA: So, where have you been?

MARY ELLEN: Well, it's been quite the afternoon.

JANINE: Coffee?

MARY ELLEN: Please.

JANINE pours MARY ELLEN a coffee.

RITA: So, what happened?

MARY ELLEN: Well, I got home from work at about one, the usual time, and I had a bite to eat, and then I put a load of laundry in . . .

VI: Well, it's Tuesday.

MARY ELLEN: That's right. So I put the laundry in and I sat down to pay some bills and out of the blue Kyle walks in the door.

VI: In the middle of the afternoon?

MARY ELLEN: That's right.

RITA: Was he sick?

MARY ELLEN: No.

JANINE: Did he get fired?

MARY ELLEN: No, nothing like that. No, I guess he felt badly about my birthday, because you know I gave them quite the tongue-lashing last night when I went home to get changed for the Cavalier.

VI: So he came home in the middle of the afternoon to apologize?

MARY ELLEN: Yes. Two o'clock in the afternoon and in he walks. It was quite the surprise.

JANINE: Two o'clock?

MARY ELLEN: Yes.

JANINE: But it's four-thirty now.

MARY ELLEN: I know.

MARY ELLEN smiles a big smile.

RITA: Oh, Mary Ellen, you didn't.

MARY ELLEN: Oh Mary Ellen did. In the dead of the afternoon. Sun shining in just as bright as can be. And I didn't care.

VI: So this was his way of making it up to you? Coming home for sex in the afternoon?

MARY ELLEN: It appears so.

VI: Isn't that just like a man? They are so narcissistic that they think having sex with us is a cure-all. And you fell for it?

MARY ELLEN: Hook, line, and sinker. Twice.

VI: Well if it was twice, that's different. That means he's actually applying himself.

MARY ELLEN: So that's why I'm late. What did I miss?

RITA: Janine's going to Halifax with Doctor Feelgood.

MARY ELLEN: What?

JANINE: I'm thinking about it. That's all. He invited me to go along with him and show him the sights and stay in separate rooms. That's it.

MARY ELLEN: Oh.

VI: Oh? That's all you have to say? Oh?

MARY ELLEN: Well, what do you want me to say?

VI: I want you to talk her out of it.

MARY ELLEN: Why?

VI: Because she already has a man at home.

MARY ELLEN: He's not at home. He's two thousand miles away.

VI: Mary Ellen?

MARY ELLEN: What?

VI: Don't you think a person should be faithful to another person even if that person is away for a while?

MARY ELLEN: I do. Definitely.

VI: There. You see?

MARY ELLEN: As long as that person is faithful in return.

VI: What?

RITA: Mary Ellen.

VI: What does that mean?

RITA: It doesn't mean anything.

JANINE: What are you saying, Mary Ellen?

MARY ELLEN: I think if you want to go to Halifax with the doctor, then go.

VI: You do not think that.

MARY ELLEN: I do.

JANINE: Mary Ellen, what's going on?

RITA: She's just had sex two times in one afternoon. She's delirious.

JANINE: Mary Ellen?

MARY ELLEN: . . . Well

RITA: Mary Ellen, don't.

MARY ELLEN: Why shouldn't I, Rita? I've been keeping this inside of me for so long it's about to give me an ulcer.

JANINE: Keeping what inside?

MARY ELLEN: He made a pass at me.

VI: Who did? The doctor?

MARY ELLEN: No.

JANINE: Bradley did?

MARY ELLEN: Yes. And he made one at Rita too.

RITA: Oh, damn it, Mary Ellen.

VI: Wait, wait. Bradley hit on you? Both of you?

MARY ELLEN: Yes.

JANINE: When did this happen?

MARY ELLEN: It happened to me last Christmas.

JANINE: Rita?

RITA: The Christmas before that.

VI: What, is this like caroling to him?

MARY ELLEN: I don't know why he did it. I just know that it took me by surprise and made me feel dirty.

JANINE: Well, what happened?

MARY ELLEN: He cornered me at Joy Bellwood's Christmas party with mistletoe in his hand. I was about to give him a little peck and he . . . well, he went a lot deeper than that. I was embarrassed and ashamed.

JANINE: I was at that party.

MARY ELLEN: I know. So was Kyle. But Bradley caught me alone in the kitchen.

VI: Oh my God.

JANINE: Oh, Mary Ellen, I'm so sorry.

VI: *(to RITA)* And what about you?

RITA: I had just bought some Christmas lights at the hardware store and I was walking home. Bradley was coming out of Dugan's and he offered to walk me. I said no, but he tagged along anyway. When we got to my place, he tried to talk me into letting him come inside, but again I said no. Then he asked me for a kiss goodnight, and before I could say no a third time he planted one on me.

JANINE: He forced himself on you?

RITA: It was a kiss. He didn't do anything else.

VI: Don't say that, Rita. He kissed you when you said no. That's a violation.

JANINE: Has he ever hit on you, Vi?

VI: Are you kidding? My Johnny's a cop. At least I hope that's the reason.

JANINE: Oh my God.

RITA: We're sorry, Janine.

JANINE: No, I'm sorry. I feel awful that he did this to my friends. Why didn't you tell me when it happened?

RITA: I just figured he'd had too much to drink and that it was a slip.

MARY ELLEN: I was too embarrassed. I didn't even tell Kyle. I only told Rita because she came into the kitchen right after it happened.

RITA: I saw that she was upset and I asked her what was wrong.

JANINE: Wow. I don't know what to say.

VI: Well, I guess this makes your decision about going to Halifax a little easier.

JANINE: Yes, it does. I don't want to have anything to do with any man after this.

VI: Actually, I thought you would be leaning in the other direction.

JANINE: I wish you had told me.

MARY ELLEN: I'm sorry.

RITA: So, what happens now?

JANINE: Now? Well, that's pretty obvious, isn't it? Now I have to rent a dumpster.

MARY ELLEN: A dumpster?

JANINE: Yes. Bradley's moving out first thing tomorrow.

SEAN enters.

VI: God. Men. They're the scourge of the earth.

RITA: They're a bunch of morons.

MARY ELLEN: Nothing but sex maniacs.

VI: Hi, Sean.

RITA: Hi, Sean.

MARY ELLEN: Hi, Sean.

SEAN: How's everyone this afternoon?

VI: Well, Sean, you've happened by at a very interesting point in the conversation, but it's not my place to enlighten you on it. I'll leave that to Janine because I know you're here for an answer to your "illicit rendezvous in Halifax" question and you're probably anxious to hear her decision, but I must tell you, you've got a harder row to hoe right now than you did ten minutes ago. Life is all about timing, isn't it? All right, ladies, let's go.

MARY ELLEN: But I haven't touched my coffee.

VI: Well, you should've gotten here sooner instead of fornicating all afternoon. Now, up you get. Rita, let's go. Have a nice chat, you two. See you tomorrow, Janine. Bye, Sean.

SEAN: Goodbye.

VI sings "Our House" as she exits.

RITA and MARY ELLEN follow her out. SEAN calls after them.

That's a Graham Nash song! That's not Neil Young!

(to JANINE) You told them that I asked you to go to Halifax with me?

JANINE: Like I said. We don't keep secrets here.

SEAN: But if you would just try.

JANINE: Sorry.

JANINE begins cleaning up.

SEAN: So, what did Vi mean by "I've got a harder row to hoe now"?

JANINE: Well, I just found out that Bradley wasn't the man I thought he was.

SEAN: Oh?

JANINE: Yes. And I'm going to be ending that relationship *tout suite.*

SEAN: It must be pretty serious, what you found out?

JANINE: It is.

SEAN: Care to share it?

JANINE: No, I think I should keep that between me and the girls.

SEAN: Oh, sure. You'll keep that a secret.

JANINE: So, that's what Vi meant when she said that.

SEAN: I see. Well, you know what? In light of this new Bradley revelation, I don't think you should go to Halifax with me.

JANINE: You don't?

SEAN: No. The important thing now is to concentrate on healing yourself. You need time. Time to sort through your feelings. You should stay here and ruminate. Be with your friends. Accept their support.

JANINE: You're right. I think that's what I'll do.

SEAN: Well, that backfired on me, didn't it? Well, I won't say I'm not disappointed, but I understand.

JANINE: Well, don't be too disappointed. I'm very fickle. Anything's possible. And you're here for another three weeks yet.

SEAN: Seventeen days to be exact.

JANINE: Until the long weekend, right?

SEAN: Right. And then I head back home.

JANINE: And what's waiting for you at home?

SEAN: Not much. Surprisingly not as much as what's here. You know, maybe I'm jealous. Maybe that's what it is.

JANINE: Jealous of what?

SEAN: Of you and the wonderful friends you have. I wish I had some of that. Maybe that's why I asked you out. Maybe I'm trying to squeeze myself into this world of yours so that I can leave mine behind.

JANINE: Or maybe you just like me.

SEAN: Or maybe it's that simple. So, we're not going to Halifax together. Could we at least have dinner sometime? Here in Stewiacke? It'll be very innocent. Above board. No expectations.

JANINE: Sounds boring.

SEAN: I like to shoot low on the first date. Then there's nowhere to go but up.

JANINE: Sure. I think we can do that.

SEAN: Good. All right, I have to go now. I've got a big night tonight.

JANINE: Do you?

SEAN: Well, it's Tuesday. Laundry. So, have a good week and let me know when you want to have that dinner.

JANINE: I will. And have a good time in Halifax.

SEAN: Oh, I'm not going to Halifax now.

JANINE: You're not?

SEAN: No, I was only going so I could spend time with you.

JANINE: Really?

SEAN: Yeah. The whole tour guide companion thing was a ruse. I just wanted to be alone with you. I had it all planned. Dinner. The theatre. Everything.

JANINE: And the staying in separate rooms idea?

SEAN: A big lie. Huge lie! No, you would fall prey to my charms and we'd wind up sleeping together. It would have been great.

JANINE: Really?

SEAN: Oh spectacular. You really missed out. But now I have to forget about all of that. I have to put those thoughts of being with you right out of my head. Ignore them completely.

JANINE: And how will you do that?

SEAN: Oh, I'll think of something.

SEAN exits singing Neil Young's "Heart Of Gold."

JANINE moves to the door and turns the sign around so that it now reads "Open" as it faces the audience. JANINE moves back into the diner. RITA appears outside the door. She knocks.

JANINE: Rita?

JANINE opens the door and lets RITA in.

What's wrong? Did you forget something?

RITA: No. No. I just . . . can we talk for a second?

JANINE: Sure we can talk. Come on in.

RITA moves into the restaurant.

RITA: Thank you. So, what was your decision? Did you tell Sean you weren't going to Halifax with him?

JANINE: Yes.

RITA: How did he take it?

JANINE: Cried like a baby. Is that what you wanted to talk about?

RITA: No, it's something else.

JANINE: Oh. Okay.

A beat as she waits for RITA to talk.

Did you want to sit?

RITA: No. No, I'm good right here.

JANINE: Do you mind if I sit?

RITA: You can do whatever the hell you like.

JANINE: Then I think I'll sit.

JANINE sits.

There that's better. I'm all set.

RITA: Right. Uh . . . Okay, here it is. There's a reason I didn't tell you when Bradley made that pass at me.

JANINE: Yes?

RITA: . . . I don't like being alone. It breaks my heart sometimes when I'm sitting at home and I'm thinking of you being with Bradley, or Vi sharing her life with Johnny, or Mary Ellen with Kyle. I know as a good friend I should be happy for the three of you but sometimes I just get overwhelmed by jealousy and sadness. I'm ashamed to admit that to you. I really am, but that's how it is sometimes. When my Shane died, Jason and I tried to carry on. We did our best to hold it together. We even talked about having another child to . . . to take Shane's place. I know how awful that sounds. But I was still young. I was only twenty-nine and I wanted children. And we could have done it. But Jason blamed himself for what happened to Shane. And even worse, he thought that I blamed him too. But I didn't, I swear. It was an accident. I know that. But Jason fell deeper and deeper into a depression and he started drinking too much, and quite frankly, Janine, I couldn't take that burden on top of losing Shane, so I left him. I took the selfish way out and I cut Jason loose without even thinking about it. And I've been afraid to get involved with anybody else since because I don't want to feel all of that pain with someone new. That scares the hell out of me. But my God it gets lonely. I feel so empty sometimes and that emptiness goes way down deep to where it seems like there's no bottom to it. To where there's no light at all. Just darkness. So, I didn't tell you about the incident with Bradley because I thought it might break you two up. And I didn't want you winding up alone like me and feeling so empty the way I do sometimes. I thought that pain would be far worse than any hurt that Bradley could cause you. And that's it. That's the God's honest truth.

JANINE: Come 'ere.

JANINE hugs RITA.

RITA: Now, let's keep this between you and me, okay? I mean, Mary Ellen and Vi think I don't give a damn about anybody but myself, and it makes them feel superior. I don't want to ruin that for them.

JANINE: My lips are sealed.

RITA: Thank you. Okay, I have to go. Things to do.

JANINE: Laundry?

RITA: Well, it's Tuesday.

RITA moves to the door then stops.

So, you're really kicking Bradley out?

JANINE: I am.

RITA: And you turned the doctor down?

JANINE: I did.

RITA: Hmm. So, now I guess we'll be alone together.

JANINE: I guess we will be.

RITA: Just you and me.

JANINE: Yep.

RITA: Well, you know what? We can sit together and watch TV at night. We can do potluck dinners with just the two of us. Go to movies together. Have pyjama parties.

JANINE: I wonder if I can still catch the doctor.

RITA: Oh, don't worry. I wouldn't do that to you. But maybe once a month we could have a night for just the two of us. You know, check in with each other. Make sure we're doing all right.

JANINE: I'd like that.

RITA: Good.

JANINE: Rita, thanks for telling me that. And I really wish you would try again with someone else. I want to see you happy.

RITA: I am happy. I've got you and Vi and Mary Ellen. I'm luckier than most. So don't worry about me. Worry about yourself. This being alone isn't for the faint of heart. It'll take some getting used to.

JANINE: Thanks for the warning, but I've been alone before.

RITA: You were alone when you were working in Montreal and travelling to all those exciting cities. You haven't been alone here, halfway to the North Pole. That's a whole different kind of alone.

RITA exits. Lights down.

SCENE TWO

Time: that Friday.

Place: the same.

Lights up. VI *and* MARY ELLEN *are sitting in the diner. The diner is closed.*

MARY ELLEN: Well, I'll tell you, Vi, it's wearing me out. I don't know how much longer I can take it.

VI: Every day at lunchtime?

MARY ELLEN: Every day this week. I get home at one o'clock and there he is waiting for me. With a big grin on his face.

VI: Can't he just wait until nighttime when you two are in bed?

MARY ELLEN: Well, it's then too!

VI: What?

MARY ELLEN: Yes! He's got this new-found vigour. He can't seem to turn it off. I mean, if the boys weren't in the house after school there'd be no downtime at all.

VI: It's that bad?

MARY ELLEN: Oh, Vi, I dropped a dishtowel last night and I was afraid to bend over to pick it up.

VI: It sounds like you've unleased a monster.

MARY ELLEN: Oh, my girl, you have no idea.

JANINE enters from the back.

VI: Did you hear this, Janine?

JANINE: Hear what?

VI: Kyle has turned into a sex machine all of a sudden.

JANINE: Really? Well, lucky you, Mary Ellen.

MARY ELLEN: Lucky? Whenever I'm alone these days I think, "Oh, that's what being motionless feels like."

JANINE: Well, you started it. You made him think you were being neglected.

MARY ELLEN: I was being neglected. I felt like a rusted-out car sitting in someone's backyard. And now I'm being waxed and buffed to within an inch of my life.

JANINE: Maybe you should be thankful. How long have you two been married?

MARY ELLEN: Twenty-one years.

JANINE: Well, I can't speak from experience, but from what I hear, sometimes that flame dies out between two people after a while.

MARY ELLEN: Well, this one's not dying. And it's not just a flame anymore. It's an out-of-control wildfire that's destroying everything in its path.

VI: Where's Rita? It's after five on a Friday. I have to go and meet Johnny.

JANINE: Maybe she got busy at the bakery.

VI: No, she's usually out of there by three at the latest.

MARY ELLEN: Has Sean been around this week, Janine?

JANINE: I haven't seen him since Tuesday.

MARY ELLEN: When you turned down his Halifax proposal.

JANINE: Right.

MARY ELLEN: Maybe you broke his spirit.

JANINE: Oh, I doubt that. He's probably just got his hands full at the clinic.

MARY ELLEN: He is a handsome one.

JANINE: Yes he is.

MARY ELLEN: Very handsome.

JANINE: Yes, I know that, Mary Ellen.

MARY ELLEN: I'm just making an observation. I didn't mean anything by it.

VI: What Mary Ellen's trying to say is, we've talked it over and we're giving you the okay to be receptive to the doctor's advances.

JANINE: Oh, are you?

MARY ELLEN: Well, it's been three days since you gave Bradley the heave-ho. Time to move on.

JANINE: Is that a suitable time to get over a guy? Three days?

VI: To get over that guy it is.

RITA enters.

There she is.

RITA: Hi.

JANINE: You're a little later than usual, Rita. We were getting worried.

RITA: Oh, I fell asleep, that's all.

MARY ELLEN: Sleep. I wish I could do that. It's getting so I'm afraid to close my eyes at my house anymore.

JANINE: Okay, now you're just bragging, Mary Ellen.

MARY ELLEN: Yeah, I am.

RITA: Bragging about what?

JANINE: Apparently Kyle can't keep his hands off of her these days.

RITA: Oh, so you've awakened the sleeping giant.

MARY ELLEN: Well, I don't know if I'd say "giant." But then, I have nothing to compare it to. Kyle's the only man I've been with.

VI: It's an expression, Mary Ellen. It's not about . . . never mind.

RITA: Well, enjoy it while you can, Mary Ellen. God, I haven't had a man since . . . Oh, no, it was last night. That's right.

JANINE: Oh cut it out!

MARY ELLEN, JANINE, and RITA laugh.

MARY ELLEN: We were just telling Janine that she has our blessing where Sean is concerned.

RITA: Oh. Good.

JANINE: You were in on the discussion too?

RITA: The three of us had a conference call last night. We were going to get together in person but Mary Ellen was tied up at home.

MARY ELLEN: Yes. That's another new wrinkle.

JANINE: Well, thank you all for your concern, but I'm just going to take it slow right now.

RITA: Suit yourself. You know what's best for you. We're only saying this because we care about you.

JANINE: And I appreciate that.

VI: Listen, everybody. I . . . uh . . . I have something to tell you.

RITA: Well, that's a mood changer. It sounds serious.

VI: Well, it is kind of serious, yes.

MARY ELLEN: Are you all right? It's not something medical, is it?

VI: No, it's nothing like that. I'm fine.

JANINE: What is it, Vi?

VI: Well . . . Johnny applied for a lateral transfer a couple of weeks ago and it's been approved.

MARY ELLEN: Lateral transfer? What does that mean?

VI: It means he's going to be moving to Thunder Bay and joining the police force there.

RITA: What?!

JANINE: Oh, Vi. No.

VI: He thinks his daughter really needs him right now. He thinks he can help her by being closer. So, he'll be moving there right away.

RITA: For how long?

VI: Well, for . . . for as long as it takes, I guess. I'm not sure. Everything is so up in the air, you know?

MARY ELLEN: I'm sorry to hear that, Vi. I know how much you love him.

VI: Oh, Mary Ellen, I love him like crazy. Like I've never loved any man.

MARY ELLEN: Oh, baby.

MARY ELLEN hugs VI.

We'll get you through this. Don't you worry.

RITA: And now there'll be three of us without partners, so you'll have lots of company. Janine, maybe you'll want to give those pyjama parties some more thought.

VI: I'm going with him.

MARY ELLEN: You're what?

VI: I'm moving to Thunder Bay with him.

JANINE: Vi, you're moving?

VI: I am. We talked it over and he wants me to come with him. And my skills are transferable, so I can set up shop anywhere. Hell, Thunder Bay is fifty times the population of Stewiacke. I'll be turning business away. So, as soon as I tie up loose ends here I'll be going out to join him. God, I can't even think straight there's so much to do.

MARY ELLEN: I can't believe you're moving.

VI: I know.

RITA: Is that why he asked you to marry him?

VI: No, that's not why.

RITA: Oh, I think it is, Vi.

VI: No, he asked me before the transfer was even approved.

JANINE: Are you going to marry him after all?

VI: I don't know. Maybe. Probably. I can't say for sure.

RITA: Well, I don't like it. I don't like you picking up and moving to Thunder Bay. Thunder Bay? Where the hell is Thunder Bay?

MARY ELLEN: Up on Lake Superior.

RITA: I know where Thunder Bay is! And I don't like it! Following a man like a little puppy dog. That's not like you, Vi. You're better than that. You're stronger than that.

VI: I'm not following him like a little puppy dog, Rita. I love him. I've shared my life with him for nine years. We're a team. And this is a decision we made together.

RITA: Well, I don't like it!

JANINE: Would you rather she stayed here, alone?

RITA: She wouldn't be alone. She's got us. You've got us, Vi. You wouldn't have to worry about being alone.

VI: I'm not worried about being alone. I'm worried about losing someone I love. You, of all people, should know why that scares me so much.

RITA: But what about the three of us? You love us.

VI: I wouldn't lose you, Rita. Or Janine or Mary Ellen. We're best friends. You don't lose best friends because you move away. We'll always be best friends.

RITA: Well, I still don't like it.

VI: Well, I don't like it either, okay? I don't like it one bit. But that's life sometimes. Sometimes life just pisses on your leg like a blind bulldog. Now, I have to go. I'm meeting Johnny. Anybody else coming?

Nobody moves.

We've only got a few of these Friday nights left, ladies. Mary Ellen? Are you coming or are you going home?

MARY ELLEN: Oh God, I'm not going home. I'm getting too much attention at home.

VI: Janine?

JANINE: Yeah, I'll be there as soon as I shut everything down here.

VI: Rita?

RITA: No, I'm not coming.

VI: Oh you are so.

RITA: I am not.

VI: Rita?

RITA: All right, yes I am, but I'm not sitting anywhere near Johnny.

VI: Oh, you will so.

RITA: All right I will, but I'm not talking to him.

VI: Oh you will too.

RITA: All right I will. But that's all I'm doing. I'm going and I'm sitting near him and I'm talking to him, but that's it!

VI: And you'll be friendly.

RITA: And I'll be friendly, but that's where it ends.

VI: We'll see you over there, Janine.

MARY ELLEN: Oh my God. I just thought of something.

VI: What?

MARY ELLEN: My birthday wish won't come true this year.

VI, MARY ELLEN, and RITA exit. Light down.

SCENE THREE

Time: Two weeks later. A Friday.

Place: the same.

Lights up. JANINE *is in the diner alone. She is sitting having a coffee. She looks at her watch.* MARY ELLEN *enters.*

JANINE: Well, finally.

MARY ELLEN: Hi, Janine.

JANINE: Everybody's late today. It's almost five.

MARY ELLEN: I know. I had a lot of errands to run and I wanted to get an early jump on them, but then Kyle came home and got an early jump on me.

JANINE: Oh God, Mary Ellen. You've become awfully crude since this new and improved sex life began.

MARY ELLEN: I have, haven't I? It's actually rather liberating.

JANINE: So, it's still going on?

MARY ELLEN: Like clockwork.

JANINE: It's been over two weeks.

MARY ELLEN: I know. And there is no let-up in sight.

JANINE: And how do you feel about that?

MARY ELLEN: Janine, I'm quite enjoying it.

JANINE: Are you?

MARY ELLEN: Oh my dear, let me tell you. At first it was exhausting because I wasn't used to it. I wasn't in condition. It's like a marathon. You have to train for it. You can't just go out and start running willy-nilly. But now that I'm in shape, well I can go the distance. And I'm not talking about a half marathon. No, girl, we're going the full twenty-six miles every time out. And we're both losing weight too because we've skipped so many lunches. No, love, there is no downside to this.

JANINE: Well, I'm glad to hear that. You sure seem rejuvenated.

MARY ELLEN: Oh, I am. I feel like a new woman.

JANINE: Would you like a coffee?

MARY ELLEN: I'll get it. You stay put. You've probably had a long day and you're not nearly in the fine shape I'm in.

MARY ELLEN goes behind the counter and pours herself a coffee.

JANINE: It was a busier lunch crowd than usual today. They didn't clear out of here until about two.

MARY ELLEN: Well, it's the long weekend. I imagine a lot of folks are taking today off too to stretch it into four days.

JANINE: Probably.

MARY ELLEN: And Johnny's leaving today. That's where Vi is. She drove him to the airport.

JANINE: Does she know when she's leaving yet?

MARY ELLEN: If she does, she hasn't told me.

JANINE: Things are really changing around here, aren't they?

MARY ELLEN: They sure are. It makes me sad, I won't lie to you. I mean, I have led an unspectacular life, Janine. In fact, some would say my life has been mundane. And I would be one of those who said it. I've lived here all of my life. I married the first man I ever dated. We raised two boys, never travelled much. Well, we went to Chicago once to see the boys play in a hockey tournament. We spent two days in a hockey rink. We might as well have been in Pugwash for all the sights we saw. My job at the preschool is nothing to write home about. It's a job that a million other women could do, and I could be replaced in a day if I ever left. I'll bet you had dreams when you were a little girl, right? Dreams of becoming someone noteworthy. Someone that did something in this life? Well, I never had those dreams. I was told early on that my future was pretty much set in stone. Finish high school, find a man, have a family. And that's what I did. I didn't become someone noteworthy. Until I started coming here, with you and Vi and Rita. Here, with you three, I feel special. I'm someone. And I'm afraid of losing that.

JANINE: You won't lose that, Mary Ellen. We're always going to be friends. And you're noteworthy on your own. You don't need us to make you feel that way.

MARY ELLEN: Thank you, love. But I do need you three to . . . Oh God, I'm going to start to get all weepy. You know me. Well, enough of that. I'll save my tears for a hard rain. That way they won't get noticed. So, what else is going on today?

JANINE: Well, it's the doctor's last day.

MARY ELLEN: Oh my God. So it is. Have you seen him at all?

JANINE: We had dinner together Wednesday night at the Cavalier.

MARY ELLEN: Yeah, I know you did.

JANINE: Then why did you ask if I'd seen him?

MARY ELLEN: I was being polite. I didn't want you to think that everybody was talking about your business even though everybody is. So, how did that go?

JANINE: It was fine. We had a nice conversation over dinner, went to Dugan's for a nightcap, and then he walked me home. He didn't even try and kiss me good night.

MARY ELLEN: The worst date of your life.

JANINE: No. It was the best. I like him, Mary Ellen. There's something about him. I like him a lot.

MARY ELLEN: Have you told him that?

JANINE: No. You see the problem is he likes me because he's on the rebound from his fiancée and now maybe I like him because I'm on the rebound from Bradley. That's way too much rebounding going on.

MARY ELLEN: Maybe you just like each other because you like each other.

JANINE: It can't be that easy, can it?

MARY ELLEN: Sometimes it is.

JANINE: Well, today's his last day so it doesn't really matter, does it?

MARY ELLEN: I don't know. You can get a lot done in one day. Just ask Kyle.

JANINE: You're bragging again.

MARY ELLEN: I most certainly am.

VI enters.

VI: Well, he's gone. I drove him to the airport, kissed him goodbye, cried a little bit, told him I loved him, cried a little bit more, and put him on the plane.

MARY ELLEN: Who are we talking about, dear?

VI: You know, I don't think Johnny and I have been apart more for more than a couple of days the whole time we've been together. This is going to be hard.

MARY ELLEN: You'll see him again soon.

VI: I know. But I swear I miss him already.

JANINE: All right, that's enough talk about men leaving.

VI: Men? What other man is leaving?

MARY ELLEN: Her doctor friend.

VI: Oh Sean, right. Have you seen him lately?

JANINE: We had dinner Wednesday.

VI: I know you did. And how was that?

MARY ELLEN: It was wonderful.

VI: Really?

MARY ELLEN: Oh, Vi, it was the best date of her life.

VI: *(to JANINE)* Well good for you. Do you think you'll see him before he goes?

MARY ELLEN: She's afraid to see him.

VI: Why?

MARY ELLEN: Well, he's on the rebound. She's on the rebound.

VI: Who cares about that?

(to JANINE) Do you like the guy?

MARY ELLEN: She does. She likes him a lot.

VI: Then that's all that matters.

MARY ELLEN: I told her that.

VI: And?

MARY ELLEN: She thinks it's too late.

VI: It's not too late. He's still here, isn't he?

MARY ELLEN: That's what I said.

VI: And?

MARY ELLEN: She still won't do anything.

VI: Well, if you're not willing to make a move then stop your whining. I'm sick of hearing you go on about it. Where's Rita?

MARY ELLEN: Don't know.

VI: Well, that's odd. Rita's usually the first one here.

JANINE: You know, she's really not taking well to the idea of you moving away, Vi.

VI: I know.

JANINE: And you're not showing her much compassion either.

VI: What do you mean?

JANINE: Well, I think Rita feels especially close to you. You're very like-minded, you two. For her, it's like losing a sister.

MARY ELLEN: For all of us it's like losing a sister.

JANINE: And I think Rita's really hurt.

VI: You're right. I guess I haven't been as thoughtful as I should be, given the circumstances.

JANINE: No, you haven't.

VI: All right. I'll try and be a little more understanding with her from now on.

RITA enters carrying a shopping bag.

RITA: Hi.

VI: Where the hell have you been?!

RITA: What's wrong?

VI: We haven't got too many of these days left, Rita. These visits we have every afternoon. You're stealing time from us by being late.

RITA: I'm sorry.

VI: Come here.

RITA: What?

VI: Give me a hug.

VI hugs RITA, crushing the shopping bag.

Oh, I love you.

RITA: Yeah, I love you too.

VI doesn't let go.

Okay, that's good, Vi. Vi. That's good.

They break the hug.

VI: So, where have you been?

RITA: I had an errand to run.

MARY ELLEN: Boy, I had errands to run today too, and I wanted to get an early jump on them, but . . .

JANINE: All right, Mary Ellen. Thank you. Coffee, Rita?

RITA: Please, Janine.

JANINE pours RITA a coffee.

VI: Okay, so now that you're all here, before you all start asking, I finally have the date that I'm going to be leaving town.

RITA: I wasn't going to ask.

MARY ELLEN: Doesn't matter to me.

JANINE: I couldn't care less.

MARY ELLEN: So, Rita, Janine had dinner with Sean on Wednesday.

RITA: Oh, I know. How was it?

JANINE: It was fine.

MARY ELLEN: It was boring.

VI: All right, all right. Very funny. Anyway, I'll be leaving two weeks tomorrow. So, there it is.

RITA: Two weeks?

VI: That's right.

MARY ELLEN: That's awfully soon, Vi.

VI: Well, I'll have all the loose ends tied up by then. I'll have everything packed and ready to go, so . . . And I don't want you throwing me a big going-away party or anything, because if you throw me a party then I'll have to make a goodbye speech in front of everybody and I wouldn't make it through it without crying, and I've cried enough these last few days and I expect I'll be doing even more crying in the next two weeks, so no party, all right?

RITA: All right.

JANINE: Fine.

MARY ELLEN: Agreed.

VI: Good . . . Really?

MARY ELLEN: Really what?

VI: I'm not getting a party?

RITA: You just said you didn't want one.

VI: Never mind what I just said. I do want a party. I want a big party. A tearful send-off. I want speeches and lots of weeping.

MARY ELLEN: I'll be weeping.

VI: I know you will, dear. We can always count on you for a good cry.

MARY ELLEN: I'm going to miss you, Vi.

VI: And I'm going to miss you too, but let's get back to the party. I want one, all right? Understood?

JANINE: Understood.

RITA: With gifts?

VI: Yes, with gifts. Going-away gifts. How can you send someone off without a gift? I want gifts.

RITA: All right, I'll get you a gift!

VI: You're damn right you will. Mary Ellen, Janine? You too. With gifts. What in the name of God were you thinking, Rita?

RITA: I'm getting you one!

VI: Well, I should hope so. Now, Janine, where the hell is my coffee? What kind of server are you, anyway? My Lord.

SEAN enters the diner.

SEAN: Good afternoon, everyone.

MARY ELLEN: Sean!

VI: Well, if it isn't the town's favourite gynecologist.

SEAN: I'm not a gynecologist.

VI: Oh? That's not what Rita said.

RITA: No, I said I wished he was.

MARY ELLEN: So, you're finished, Sean. Your tenure in Stewiacke is completed.

SEAN: It is. And I am sorry to see my time here come to an end. As you know, when I came here I was at a low point in my life.

RITA: You were a pitiful sight.

VI: Oh, my boy, you were draggin' ass.

SEAN: Yes. But thanks in no small part to you four ladies, I am charting my way out of that morbid abyss.

MARY ELLEN: I love the way he talks.

SEAN: So, I want to thank you. In fact, I want to show you how much improvement I've made since coming here. Rita, did you get what I asked you to get?

RITA: I sure did.

RITA reaches into her shopping bag and takes out a music player and sets it on the counter.

VI: What's going on?

SEAN: For the last ten days Rita and I have been meeting secretly.

MARY ELLEN: Really?!

SEAN: No, it's nothing like that.

RITA: Not for a lack of trying on my part.

VI: You do go the extra mile.

RITA: I told him that. His answer was still no.

SEAN: Anyway, as I was saying, Rita has been giving me dancing lessons.

JANINE: What?!

SEAN: That's right.

MARY ELLEN: Well, hello for goin'.

SEAN: Yes. Well, I don't know what that means, but apparently women like a man who can dance. At least, that's what I'm told.

JANINE: *(to RITA)* You didn't tell me you were giving him dancing lessons.

RITA: He asked me to keep it a secret.

SEAN: *(to JANINE)* You see? It's that easy. And so, if you will permit me. Rita?

RITA turns on the music player. We hear a song, possibly "Woodstock" by Crosby, Stills, Nash, and Young.

SEAN holds out his hand to JANINE.

Janine? May I have this dance?

MARY ELLEN and VI ooooh and ahhh. JANINE steps forward and takes SEAN's hand. They begin to dance to the song.

RITA: Head up, Sean. Keep that back straight.

After a moment of dancing, he yells above the music.

SEAN: How am I doing?!

JANINE: I'm very impressed!

They continue dancing. After a moment or two MARY ELLEN, VI, and RITA join in dancing as well. After a little more of the dancing, SEAN goes to the music player and turns it off.

VI: Hey!

RITA: What are you doing?

JANINE: Is that it?

MARY ELLEN: I was just getting revved up.

SEAN: Always leave them wanting more, right?

JANINE: Well, I do want more.

SEAN: You do?

JANINE: I do, sir.

SEAN: Then come to Halifax with me this weekend.

JANINE: What?

SEAN: Come to Halifax with me and we'll dance.

JANINE: I thought you were going home.

SEAN: There's nothing for me at home. Why should I be in a rush to get back there? There's a lot more for me right here.

JANINE: Like what?

SEAN: You.

MARY ELLEN, RITA, and VI ooooh!

And don't tell me I'm on the rebound again because I'm not. I realize now that having my engagement broken off was a good thing. Rebecca wasn't the woman for me. It was wrong from the start. I know that now. And I know that because of meeting you and seeing the kind of woman you are. I like who you are, Janine. Hell, I think you're bloody spectacular. I like the way you make me feel. I like the way my stomach jumps when I know I'm going to see you. I like thinking about what it would be like to hold your hand. To put my arm around your waist. To get lost in those eyes. To kiss those lips. And even if those events never come to pass—if that good fortune never smiles on me—the mere thought of them will have been pleasure enough.

VI: Oh, girls, did you hear that?

MARY ELLEN: That's the most beautiful thing I've ever heard any man say.

RITA: I don't mind telling you, I am more than just a little aroused.

SEAN: Come with me, Janine. You don't want me wandering the streets of Halifax alone, do you? All hangdog. All woebegone. And if I don't go with you, who else am I going to go with?

RITA raises her hand.

RITA: Uh. I . . . could . . .

VI pulls RITA's hand down.

SEAN: What do you say, Janine?

She doesn't answer.

Come on. Don't tell me those dancing lessons were for nothing.

JANINE: All right, I'll go to Halifax with you, Doctor Merrit.

VI, MARY ELLEN, and RITA applaud and shout "Yay!"

But, just as your tour guide.

SEAN: Agreed.

JANINE: We'll see the sights, have dinner, go to the theatre, go dancing, sleep together, and come straight home.

SEAN: Really?

JANINE: All right, we don't have to go to the theatre.

SEAN: What?

JANINE: I'm kidding. I love the theatre.

SEAN: Okay, then. So, I'll pick you up when? About an hour?

JANINE: No. We'll leave tomorrow morning. Friday nights are for me and my girlfriends. And we don't have too many Fridays left. Right, girls?

VI: That's right.

MARY ELLEN: No, we don't.

RITA: Nope.

SEAN: I understand completely. We'll leave first thing tomorrow morning then.

JANINE: I look forward to it. Oh, and, Sean? I was kidding about sleeping together.

SEAN: Of course you were.

JANINE: We'll need separate rooms.

SEAN: I knew that.

JANINE: Did you?

SEAN: Absolutely. I mean, agreeing to have sexual relations in advance like that would make the intimacy too casual. Meaningless. Who would do that?

RITA raises her hand. VI pulls RITA's hand down.

All right, ladies. I hope you have a wonderful evening.

VI: We will.

RITA: We always do.

SEAN: Thanks for everything, Rita.

RITA: You're welcome.

RITA gives SEAN a hug.

VI: Save some of that lovin' for me, mister. Come on.

SEAN gives VI a hug.

There you go.

SEAN gives MARY ELLEN a hug.

MARY ELLEN: Sean? You've performed a minor miracle here. You know that?

SEAN: How so?

MARY ELLEN: You've made us believe that folks from Toronto aren't so bad after all.

SEAN: Thank you, Mary Ellen. Oh, your niece Martine was at the clinic today. She has an ear infection.

MARY ELLEN: Your stethoscope??

SEAN: A photo of my ex-fiancée.

MARY ELLEN: I'll tell her to bring it back.

SEAN: No. Tell her she can keep it.

SEAN exits.

MARY ELLEN: I'm going to miss him.

VI: Oh, something tells me we haven't seen the last of Doctor Sean Merrit. Right, Janine?

JANINE: You never know.

VI: All right, come on. That beer at Dugan's isn't going to drink itself.

RITA: Wait. Can I say something?

VI: Can it wait until we get to the bar?

RITA: No, I want to say it now with just the four of us here. It's about the changes we're all going through. I mean, Janine will be off to Halifax tomorrow with a new man; Vi, you're moving thousands of miles away to start a new life; Mary Ellen is a sexual revolution in sensible shoes. I just want you to know that I'm happy for the three of you. I'm genuinely happy.

VI: . . . That's it?

RITA: That's it.

VI: Well, we know you're happy for us, Rita. You're our friend. Of course you're happy for us.

RITA: I just wanted to say it.

JANINE: Thank you, Rita.

VI: All right, let's go.

MARY ELLEN: Wait.

VI: Oh, what now?

MARY ELLEN: Just a little more.

JANINE: A little more what?

MARY ELLEN turns the music on again. VI, RITA, JANINE, and MARY ELLEN dance.

Lights down.

End.

Norm Foster has been the most produced playwright in Canada every year for the past twenty years. His plays receive an average of one hundred and fifty productions annually. Norm has over sixty plays to his credit, including *The Foursome*, *On a First Name Basis*, and *Hilda's Yard*. He is the recipient of the Los Angeles Drama-Logue Award for his play *The Melville Boys* and is an Officer of the Order of Canada. He lives in Fredericton.

First edition: April 2021
Printed and bound in Canada by Rapido Books, Montreal

Cover art and design by Patrick Gray Illustration

PLAYWRIGHTS
CANADA PRESS
202-269 Richmond St. W.
Toronto, ON
M5V 1X1

416.703.0013
info@playwrightscanada.com
www.playwrightscanada.com
@playcanpress